# NOVARODOK

# NOVARODOK

## A Movement That Lived in Struggle
### and
## Its Unique Approach to the Problem of Man

MEIR LEVIN

JASON ARONSON INC.
*Northvale, New Jersey*
London

This book was set in 11 pt. Goudy Oldstyle by Alpha Graphics of Pittsfield, New Hampshire.

Copyright © 1996 by Meir Levin

10  9  8  7  6  5  4  3  2

All rights reserved. Printed in the United States of America. No part of this book may be used or reproduced in any manner whatsoever without written permission from Jason Aronson Inc. except in the case of brief quotations in reviews for inclusion in a magazine, newspaper, or broadcast.

**Library of Congress Cataloging-in-Publication Data**

Levin, Meir, 1960-
   Novarodok : a movement that lived in struggle and its unique approach to the problem of man / Meir Levin.
     p. cm.
   Includes bibliographical references.
     ISBN: 978-1-56821-603-4

   1. Hurwitz, Joseph, of Navaradok, d. 1919.  2. Musar movement.
3. Judaism—Belarus—Novogrudok—History.  4. Rabbis—Belarus—Novogrudok—Biography.  5. Ethics, Jewish.  I. Title.
BM755.H83L48  1996
296.8'3—dc20

96-11264

Manufactured in the United States of America. Jason Aronson Inc. offers books and cassettes. For information and catalog write to Jason Aronson Inc., 230 Livingston Street, Northvale, New Jersey 07647.

מי זה האיש ירא ה', יורנו בדרך יבחר (תהילים כה,יב)

בס"ד

# TALMUDICAL YESHIVA OF PHILADELPHIA

6063 Drexel Road
Philadelphia, Pennsylvania 19131
215 - 477 - 1000

Rabbi Elya Svei
Rabbi Shmuel Kamenetsky
Roshei Yeshiva

November 27, 1995

Dear Reb Meir אי"ה

    After perusing your manuscript, I have come to admire your undertaking. It is surely a very responsible pursuit which has a great potential for helping ישראל כלל.

    The life of the Alter of Novardok was a living "Mussar Sefer". By studying his way of life the reader is inspired to emulate his Madragas Haadom.

    Your idea to have the book reviewed by the descendents of the Alter is a great enhancement. They are the direct link in his path of life.

    May it be His will that you should accomplish your goal to be שבע רצון הבורא with this endeavor.

Sincerely yours,

Rabbi Shmuel Kamenetsky
Dean

RSK:sm

## ישיבה דרך איתן ע״ש מרן רבי אברהם יפהן זצ״ל
## Derech Ayson Rabbinical Seminary/Yeshiva of Far Rockaway

802 HICKSVILLE ROAD, FAR ROCKAWAY, NEW YORK 11691 • 718-327-7600

Rabbi Yechiel I. Perr
*Rosh Yeshiva*

Rabbi Aaron M. Brafman
*Menahel*

Rabbi Eli Goldgrab
*General Studies Principal*

בס״ד

"Novarodok" is an authentic presentation of Novarodok Musor; and as such, it is a most important contribution to the field of Musor writings. It is also a powerful work, and indeed a moving work, and it may well become a classic. It is significant that it comes at a time of renewed interest in Musor in general, and of Novarodok Musor in particular.

I think that it is important to point out that, although Novarodok Musor was unique in its focus on doing and on not compromising, at the same time it was by no means unique in its philosophical underpinnings. A study of the writings of the Gaon of Vilna, especially his commentary to Mishlei, will disclose much of the origin of Madregos Ha'adam. And an examination of the writings of the Chafetz Chaim will elicit many parallels to Novarodok Musor. The student of this work need not be concerned that he is following some "extremist" ideas in Avodas Hash-m. In fact, the opposite is true. Following the teachings of Madragos Ha'adam will inspire a person to climb ever upwards to greater self perfection.

My wish for the author is that he witness the fulfillment of the prayer of King David, "And may the pleasantness of Hash-m be upon us: And the work of our hands be established for us; indeed, the work of our hands be His establishment."

Rabbi Yechiel Yitzchok Perr

# Contents

Foreword     xi
Introduction     xiii

**Part I—The Coat of Many Colors**

1  The Beginnings     3
2  The Yeshiva in Novarodok     11
3  The Storming of the Soul     13
4  The Years of Trouble     21
5  The Revolution     27
6  The Next Generation     33
7  The House of Joseph in Poland     37
8  Flight and Rebirth     43

**Part II—Selections from *Madreigas Ho'odom***

9  Introduction     49
10  The Epochs     55
     The First Man     55
     Noach and the Generation of the Flood     58
     The Times of our Father Avraham     60

|   |   |
|---|---|
| The Revelation at Sinai | 64 |
| The Prophets | 70 |
| The Era of the Yeshivas | 71 |
| 11 From: Correcting Character Traits | 79 |
| 12 From: The Paths of *Bitachon* | 83 |
| 13 From: The Ways of Life | 93 |
| 14 From: Leading the Many to Righteousness | 99 |

## Part III—Rav Yosef Yozel's Life and Teachings

|   |   |
|---|---|
| 15 The Legacy of Rav Yosef Yozel | 105 |
| 16 The Sayings of Rav Yosef Yozel | 125 |

## Part IV—The Next Generation

|   |   |
|---|---|
| 17 Rav Avrohom Jofen | 137 |
| 18 Rav Avrohom Zalmanes | 141 |
| 19 Rav Dovid Bliacher | 143 |
| 20 Rav Dovid Budnik | 145 |
| 21 Rav Yisroel Yakov Lubchansky | 149 |
| 22 Rav Mordechai Shimanovits | 153 |
| 23 Rav Yoel Baranchik | 155 |
| 24 Rav Yitzhak Elchonon Valdshein | 157 |
| 25 Rav Shraga Magid | 161 |
| 26 Rav Nisan Bobruisker | 163 |
| Appendix I: Novarodok Philosophy of History | 167 |
| Appendix II: The Yeshiva Schedule | 169 |
| Appendix III: Novarodok Battle Song | 171 |
| Glossary | 173 |
| Bibliography | 179 |

# Foreword

When asked to write this foreword, I remarked that my comments cannot merely reflect my reaction to this book. They must reflect my reaction to the essence of its topic—the Musar of Novarodok.

As a great grandchild of the legendary Rav Yozel, I have worn this crown called Novarodok my whole life. Sometimes it sat regally, high upon my head; sometimes it hung like an albatross around my neck.

This ancestry undoubtedly has had a profound influence upon my life and style. Somehow, I have always felt swirling around me, the tempestuous winds of the eternal, internal war of the soul that Novarodok addresses so relentlessly. I knew that, whereas other branches of the Musar movement believed in "working on the soul," Novarodok had disdain for such an approach. Novarodok believed in "storming the soul." That is the essence of Rav Yozel's teachings.

In 1968 I contemplated studying *Kodoshim* (tractates of the Talmud that deal with the Temple service) at the Brisk Yeshiva in Jerusalem, under the tutelage of Rabbi Berel Soloveitchik. Brisk yeshivas have traditionally shared the anti-musar sentiment that pervaded certain Lithuanian citadels of learning. I asked my grandfather, the hallowed *Rosh Yeshiva* of Novarodok, Rav Avrohom Jofen, if he would consider that a betrayal of my Musar roots.

After a few pensive moments, he replied that I may indeed study at the Brisk Yeshiva. However, he continued, it is imperative that I first absorb the following message, for the difference between Brisk and Novarodok must be clearly understood.

The Talmud tells us in *Shabbos* (133b): "This is my God and I will beatify him—this means, make him beautiful with *mitzvos*. Make before him a beautiful *succah*, a beautiful *lulav*, a beautiful *shofar*, a beautiful *tallis*, a beautiful Torah scroll. Abba Shoul says: 'To beatify Him"—to be like Him. Just as God is merciful and compassionate, so too should you be merciful and compassionate.'"

This passage puts forth two distinct ways of "beatifying" the Almighty. That is the difference between Brisk and Novarodok. The ultimate goal of both is glorification of God's name. However, the two schools pursue this holy purpose in two disparate ways.

Brisk emphasizes the visible, external manifestations of *mitzvah* performance as the means of sanctifying God's name. Novarodok, on the other hand, places its focus on the internal perfection of character traits by emulating Divine Truth and Compassion.

"Just remember, my child," said my grandfather, "if you sincerely intend to glorify God's name, remember that the Rambam rules according to the opinion of Abba Shoul" (*Deyos* 1, 6).

To beatify our Master, to elevate the *Kvod Shemaim* by climbing higher and higher up the ladder of *Madreigas Ho'odom*—this is the glory of Novarodok.

—Rabbi Moshe Faskowitz,
Rabbi of Congregation Torah
Center of Hillcrest
President of the Council of Rabbis
of National Council of Young Israel

# Introduction

What is Musar and what is Novarodoker Musar? This question goes to the heart of this book. In its resolution centers the understanding of the Jewish spiritual quest. As Jews, we look to the struggles of the past for guidance and inspiration. Novarodok has much to teach us in this regard.

A simple and approximate definition of Musar must include its emphasis on ethics, its roots in talmudic learning, and its psychological underpinnings. As Musar philosophy and approach unfolded, it took on complexity and luster. It was multifaceted, spiritually vibrant and intense, and reflected an authentic Jewish response to the intellectual, physical, and spiritual dislocations of the modern age. In essence, it was an affirmation and a restatement of the eternal values of an eternal people.

The Musar movement arose in the latter part of the nineteenth century in Jewish Lithuania, with Rav Yisroel Salanter and his disciples, and soon provoked intense opposition. At the root of the disagreement lay basic philosophical differences. Some opponents thought that the Musar approach consisted only of a set of behaviors and conventions that, even if well-intentioned, were simply not necessary. They did not see the fire that burned within. Others subscribed to the view that Judaism demands a remaking of the personality through the study of Torah alone. According to this viewpoint, total commitment to the intense discipline of study and immersion in the give-and-take of talmudic discourse, by itself and without the need for any additional effort, changes the very nature of man and transforms and links him to the Divine. Spending extended periods of time in ethical reflection and training, they thought, is superfluous and a distraction. Yet others acted from the misconception that a good Jew punctiliously keeps the commandments and studies Torah and that this is all God asks of man. The issue, however, ran deeper.

Lithuanian Jewry saw its Torah through the prism of the teachings of the Vilna Gaon. This remarkable personality defined the direction of the nonchasidic world for two hundred years through his profundity of thought, breadth of knowledge, and clear spiritual vision. For him, Judaism rested on the triune foundation of Torah, *Middos*, and *Mitzvos*. These elements were unified in his thinking, but for his disciples, these concepts began to diverge. The mighty river of the Gaon's teachings now flowed in several channels.

Rav Chaim of Volozhin emphasized the aspect of his teacher's philosophy that has been rightly called *Torah Lishmo*, "Torah for its own sake." To him, in practice no less than in theory, Torah was the source of the world, the blueprint for reality, an early emanation of God's indescribable essence. Torah is greater than man, world, society. The universe is but a pale reflection of Torah's grandeur. "Delve into it and delve into it, for everything is in it"(*Avos* 5, 25). Torah study is the vehicle for Divine revelation in the material world; nay, it is itself that revelation. All other concerns of humankind fade into insignificance when compared with Torah.

No one disputed that the Musar works of previous generations were valuable and should be studied. For Volozhin, they were a useful adjunct to intensive Torah study. In fact, attaining good character is indispensable to retaining one's Torah knowledge. Rav Chaim Volozhiner compared *Yiras Shemaim* to a silo and Torah learning to a harvest. Without a silo to store it, the harvest will rot and be lost. But a silo without a harvest is not even a silo (*Nefesh Hachaim* 4, 8). Those who held this view believed that Torah study itself elevates those who occupy themselves with it. Above all, man's task in this world is to learn Torah, for it is greater than all created things. The unfolding of this approach culminated in the famous scholarly dynasty of Brisk.

Musar inherited the other side of the Gaon's teachings. It traces its origin through Rabbi Yisroel Salanter to Reb Zundel of Salant and to *his* teacher, Rav Chaim Volozhiner, and thus to the Gaon of Vilna himself. As Rav Yisroel Salanter saw it, Musar and Torah study are part of one another but they are also separate and distinct. Musar study devolves even on women who are exempt from the requirement to study theoretical portions of the Torah. On the other hand, directed study of areas of *Halachah* that deal with Musar obligations is an absolute prerequisite to spiritual progress. For a true Musar personality, there is no sharp boundary. What, after all, is Musar, if not application of advanced techniques of Torah learning—deep and penetrating analysis, insightful and novel reasoning, exact classification and incessant review, to the substratum of the human soul. Authentic Musar study can only be accomplished by a scholar of substantial ability and erudition and only after years of effort and growth. It broadens the subjects under inquiry, addresses the human condition, searches for the truth as it pertains to emotions and behavior, and applies the truth to personal goals. This process is predominantly guided by insights into the Bible, the Talmud, the Midrash, and related literature. Nevertheless, there was a subtle shift of emphasis. Musar insisted that the world was created for man to pursue perfection. Torah knowledge is indispensable to this goal, aside from its own great intrinsic value, and it joins man in the center of the universe. "Man is required to say every day: 'For me, the world was created'" (*Sanhedrin* 37a).

Consequently, the question "What is man's duty in this world?" is the central question of life, for an individual as well as for society.

Musar brought into the open and made explicit this very inquiry. Its followers changed the very terms of the religious discourse. Musar based itself on the bedrock of traditional teachings but suffused them with a new light and understanding. It restored the basics that were being forgotten and turned to oppose and dispute the assumptions of the "enlightened." This movement fueled the development of yeshivas as a means to propagate Torah knowledge and practice and, in this fashion, retarded the advancement of *Haskalah*. Musar developed a philosophy of self-education and raised to the forefront of religious life the awareness of oneself, one's psyche, and one's place in the world as the prerequisite for and the battleground of spiritual advancement. Musar made explicit what was previously assumed and thus carried its message to the wider community.

There were as many types of Musar as there were Musar masters; after all, Rabbi Yisroel Salanter himself expected each man and woman to apply Musar teachings to his or her own unique circumstances. He counseled his students to pursue the way that fit them best. The stress on individual development remained a source of strength, as well as a limitation, for the movement as a whole, because this approach could not be easily generalized and popularized for mass consumption. There were, nevertheless, three main currents that eventually did predominate and produce leaders and scholars. One could almost tell which student came from what institution by his behavior, patterns of thought, and demeanor. Slobodka brought forth refined, aristocratic, luminescent personalities, each in full Divine image and each in his own likeness. It focused on the greatness of man and on the immeasurable potential of each person. The Alter of Slobodka demonstrated that the Torah views human beings as God's direct handiwork and as His personal concern. The Alter taught that conventional understanding of ethical and spiritual concepts is superficial and shallow and ultimately unworthy. In his *shmuessen*, he demonstrated that Torah's conceptions of gratitude, honor, kindness and many other human qualities are remarkably pure and profound, sublime and elevated beyond our everyday understanding. Slobodka took a student beyond his personal limitations and thus lifted him out of the field of battle and into the rarefied regions of spiritual greatness. It drew a young student toward an ideal that captured his imagination and changed his deepest aspirations. There was no need to struggle with oneself. By the time the Alter of Slobodka caught a boy's soul, he turned into an elevated man—for he desired only elevated things. The Alter was a consummate pedagogue whose mastery and knowledge of human nature were unsurpassable. He raised an entire generation of leaders who, each in his own way, carried the vision of man's greatness into subsequent generations. The Alter motivated and led, inspired and taught, influenced and innovated. Many Torah leaders of our times were molded in Slobodka.

Kelm was elemental, comprehensive, and encyclopedic. The Alter of Kelm was a direct inheritor of Rav Yisroel Salanter and, like him, a man of detail. Kelm stressed discipline, harmony, order, organization, and control. Kelm valued the power of concentration and produced calm, rational, ordered individuals who were at peace with themselves and others, whose piety interdigitated with all aspects of their environment, whose intelligence led them because they so accustomed themselves. Rav Simcha Zissel Ziv left behind a body of insights that were subsequently developed into a coherent system of teachings. These focused on a wide range of Musar ideas and promoted a balanced development of personality.

In Kelm, as in Slobodka, one sought *shleimus*. This term is usually translated as "completeness," but it means more, much more. *Shleimus* intimates harmony and balance and a welding of intellect and emotion into a new spiritual entity. Musar taught one how and when to rejoice and how and when to cry. What is more important, it explained how to be joyful and when not to cry. This is an important point—Musar was a practical discipline that showed one how to accomplish exalted goals. In Kelm one saw and lived side by side with those who had already accomplished these goals. The Alter of Slobodka and the Alter of Novarodok measured their emerging paths by Kelm's standard.

This book is about Novarodok, a revolutionary development. It was radical and uncompromising to the point of excluding other views; it demanded total commitment and it was immensely successful. Novarodok demanded constant tension and critical self-analysis. Struggle against every weakness and affirmation of man's imperfection were the core of its message. Inner tension, not harmony, was its daily bread or, more accurately, its daily medicine. Directed release of impulse and feeling, not their subordination to the intellect, was the key to its success against overwhelming odds. To a Novarodoker, Musar was a powerful antidote, a cure for the sickness within. Not to make the existent self perfect, but to tear it down and rebuild it, in the never-ending struggle for perfection—that is man's occupation in this world. This was not a philosophy for lazybodies.

It is important to emphasize at this point that all branches of the Musar movement eschewed reflexive piety and spiritual asceticism. Sadness and melancholy were to be avoided. The Alter of Slobodka refused to accompany a certain scholar on a trip because that individual never smiled. Grim self-abnegation is foreign to the spirit of Musar. The task of molding oneself into the true image of God does not allow squandering of inner resources through depression or hostility. Every talent and every strength of personality must be recruited to the ultimate goal of reaching greatness. Novarodok was intense but in its heart lay a striving for purity and a longing for spiritual beauty and grandeur.

Novarodok produced *Madreigas Ho'odom*, the only comprehensive text of Musar literature. Novarodok stressed feeling and creativity. Its teachings combined talmudic rigor with deep psychological insight; it was practical and "hands on." Novarodok was a program of action, a network, and a fellowship. Novarodok institutions endowed a tightly cohesive group of adherents with the strength and courage to face down the Communist revolution. The movement grew and expanded in the most harrowing of circumstances.

In its mildest form, Musar is a set of teachings and insights into the soul of the Torah and the teachings of its sages. In fact, this is how it is now commonly perceived. However, Novarodok was more than this. Novarodok was an all-consuming fire, its teachings were flames, its atmosphere electric. The image and terminology of fire and conflagration are omnipresent in its literature. Novarodok faced down and rejected modernity, for it perceived the perverseness in modern man's heart and, more importantly, in his reasoning. The movement militantly opposed the corruption that seeped into the Holy and set up in its path a wall of fire. This Musar school was unique and it has much to teach us.

# Introduction

The world has changed. The ideal of "progress" has shown its true face, the face of inhumanity and degradation. The idols have toppled and the axioms of yesterday have revealed their emptiness. Novarodok carried the banner of Torah-true Judaism into the heat of battle. Its insights apply now no less than they did seventy years ago. The story of its heroism can inspire us. Its commitment can lead us. We also can catch its fire. For the modern day seeker, this book has been written.

\* \* \*

One who attempts to translate the teachings of the founder of the Novarodok movement, Rav Yosef Yozel, faces an almost insurmountable challenge. The *Madreigas Ho'odom* is a transcription of Rav Yosef Yozel's talks and reflects his conversational style. It comprises single sentence paragraphs that freely mix persons and tenses and sometimes occupy whole pages of text. The ideas are profound and presuppose intimate familiarity with both the talmudic and the Musar literature.

I have elected, therefore, to break up these sentences and to employ transitional devices to make the translation idiomatically correct and intelligible to English speakers. At times, abridgement was necessary to bring out the true flavor of the original. The Rambam says, in his letter to Shmuel Ibn Tibbon:

> A great principle, that anyone who wishes to translate from one language to another and endeavors to translate word for word, and keeps the order of the statements and the arrangement of the words, will wear himself out and come to a confusing and inaccurate translation. It is not proper to do so. But he must translate primarily the content so that the meaning is clear and then elaborate upon what is derived from it in the tongue of the translation. This is not possible unless he creates introductions and summaries and clarifies one word in many and many words in one.

In taking this advice, I follow Novarodok precedent.[1]

---

1. Introduction to *Torás Yitshak*.

The length of the Rav Yosef Yozel's work, *Madreigas Ho'odom*, makes accurate translation of its totality a much greater project that I can properly accomplish. In addition, my goal is merely to introduce the English-speaking public to Novarodok and to promote further study into this phenomenon. I have therefore elected to present the biography of the founder of the movement, Rav Yosef Yozel, for his life represents the truths of Novarodok in their purest summation. This is followed by selections from *Madreigas Ho'odom*, recollections and aphorisms.

Novarodok was a movement. Many other spiritual heroes labored, sacrificed, and promoted the Musar of Novarodok. There are published Torah thoughts by nearly sixty individuals. Properly presenting all of these great men is outside the scope and intent of this work. I have selected the teachings of certain leaders of the movement's many offshoots and have presented these in the second part of the book. My goal is to introduce the variety and richness of their thought and to show the present-day reader what was lost in the destruction of the Holocaust. The selection is therefore very personal and weighted toward those teachers active in the prewar period.

I am fully cognizant that the responsibility for the format of this book and for all errors rests with me alone. I have attempted to remove them by submitting the book to review by experts. Still, the possibility for misunderstanding greatly concerns me. The reader should view this effort as an introduction to the many profound ideas and teachings that were Novarodok and should refer to the originals for further study.

* * *

My greatest appreciation goes to Rabbi Chaim Boruch Faskowitz and Rabbi Shlomo Margolis for first introducing me to the thought of Novarodok. I thank Rabbi Moshe Faskowitz for kindly lending me *seforim* from his library and for his support and advice. Rabbi Yechiel Y. Perr offered comments and suggestions on almost every page and paragraph. This help was invaluable and is deeply appreciated. Mr. Paul Adler rescued the manuscript when the computer's hard drive crashed. I thank my parents for bequeathing to me the qualities and dreams that made this work imaginable. Most importantly I thank my dear wife, Chaya, for her advice and for her support, which afforded me the time and opportunity to make it possible. I couldn't have done it otherwise. Above all, I thank Ribbono Shel Olam for all His generosity—"who am I and what is my house that You have brought me to this point" (1 Samuel 7:18). May His kindness remain with us forever.

# I
# The Coat of Many Colors

# 1
# The Beginnings

Rabbi Yosef Yozel Hurvitz is reported to have been born in 1847 or 1850. His father, Rav Shlomo Zalman Ziv (later changed to Hurvitz), was a *Dayan* of Polanga, a town on the shores of the Baltic sea, and later a Rav in Kortobin, near Shauli, Lithuania. Rav Shlomo Zalman was a man known for his piety and total immersion in Torah study and his *rebbetzin* was renowned for her charitable endeavors. The family lived next to the *Beis Midrash* and the house was wide open to rabbis, *maggidim*, and yeshiva students who passed through the town. As did other rabbis of small towns in Lithuania, Rabbi Shlomo Zalman lived in physical poverty but surrounded by innumerable spiritual riches.

Rabbi Shlomo Zalman taught his sons by himself. Besides Torah, he taught them the proper ways of behavior, taking care to individualize this instruction to fit each son's temperament and inclinations. His son Yosef Yozel was a strong-willed and courageous boy. As a small child, he fought off a large vicious dog belonging to the Polish landowner, which harassed the local citizens. The father's efforts bore fruit and at sixteen Yosef Yozel began to give lectures in the *Beis Midrash* in Kortobin and in Kelm.

At a young age he was betrothed to the oldest daughter of Yakov Shtein from Sveksena, a town on the German–Lithuanian border. Reb

Yakov died before the marriage and the young scholar accepted responsibility for the widow and eight children, rather than break off the engagement. After the marriage, Reb Yozel took over the management of his father-in-law's textile store and the business prospered.

Despite his many responsibilities, the young scholar continued to study Torah and delivered lectures in the local *Beis Midrash*. After obtaining sufficient profit each day, he closed the store and hastened to the study hall. Eventually, he decided to bring his wares to Memel (now Klaipeda). This promised a higher profit margin and more time for Torah.

During one of these visits, he made an acquaintance with Rav Yisroel Salanter,[1] who then lived in Memel. It is likely that the founder of Musar recognized the talents and abilities of this young merchant and tried to influence him. Rav Salanter stopped Reb Yozel during a particularly hectic trading day and asked him, "Why do you rush so much?" "I have to support a large family," he replied. The elder rabbi countered that one must still set aside most of one's time for Torah. The conversation that followed forged a bond between them and Reb Yosef Yozel began to attend Rav Yisroel's lessons in *Mesilas Yeshorim*. He heard thirteen lectures and, with each, Yosef Yozel's longing for a life dedicated to Torah and *Yiras Shemaim* grew. After the last of these lectures, he became determined to completely change his life.

---

1. A different version of their first meeting has Rav Yosef Yozel entering Rav Yisroel's House of Study to "talk Torah." Other sources state that this meeting was arranged by Rabbi Eliahu of Katrina. Rav Yisroel asked Yosef Yozel whether he had a coach waiting. When the latter responded affirmatively, Rav Yisroel told him that he must not cause the coachman to tarry, for one is not permitted to cause another to suffer even to increase his own Torah knowledge. Yosef Yozel was very impressed and returned again to seek out Rav Yisroel and to attend his lectures. In Rabbi Pesach Crohn's *In the Footsteps of the Magid* (ArtScroll, 1992), another version is reported. In this variant, it was Rav Yitshak Blaser who asked Yosef Yozel, "Why are you in such a hurry?" Rav Yosef Yozel answered that he had to work in order to earn a living for himself and his family. Rav Blaser reportedly retorted: "But one must also know how to prepare to die"(Compare *Tamid* 32a).

# The Beginnings

When he returned home, Reb Yosef Yozel appeared uninterested in business matters. When the time came to replenish his stocks, he made no special efforts to do so. When his family questioned him about this, he consented to travel to Memel but told them that this was to be his last trip. Midway there, however, he reconsidered. He returned, gave his money pouch to his mother-in-law (who subsequently managed the business), and left, in order to dedicate himself to a life of Torah and Musar.[2]

Rav Yisroel Salanter attempted to dissuade his recent pupil from a decision that jeopardized his family's means of support. He prevailed upon Yosef Yozel to seek counsel from his father, the aged Rav of Kortobin. Reb Yozel agreed to do so, although in his heart the decision was final. His father was appalled and strongly opposed his son's course of action. Reb Yosef Yozel refused to comply. To strengthen his resolve, he vowed never to return to Kortobin and later forswore all of his father's possessions.[3]

Rav Yosef Yozel considered traveling to Warsaw to attend lectures of Rabbi Yosef Dov Soloveitchik, the *Beis Halevi*. He finally decided to remain closer to Rav Yisroel Salanter[4] and joined the circle of the latter's students in Kovno who two years later were gathered together as the nucleus of the famed Kovno Kollel. The most prominent of these were Rav Naftoli Amsterdam, Rav Yitshak Blaser and Rav Avrohom Shenker. Yosef Yozel was then twenty-seven years old.[5]

The *kollel* was supported by the noted sponsor of Musar Reb Shraga Frank, himself an exemplary ethical personality. It served as an incubator for Musar ideas and there, in its rarefied atmosphere of spiritual idealism, the future leaders of the Musar movement developed themselves.

---

2. See Hoemek Davar by Netsiv of Volozhin on Genesis 12:4–5.
3. The Mitzvah of Talmud Torah precedes the requirement to obey one's father. (*Yore Deah* 240, 13).
4. Rav Yisroel lived for several years in Kovno, where he established a nucleus for the future movement. He often returned there subsequently to inspire and direct his followers.
5. Twenty-five, according to some sources.

For Rav Yosef Yozel, this was a time of great sacrifice and great growth. At times he would leave Kovno to wander anonymously around Jewish Lithuania, seeking self-improvement and purification through exile. During one such episode, he signed on as an unpaid *shames* in the outlying town of Romshishek. There, for three months, in complete anonymity, he strived to transform and remake his character traits. One night a visiting rabbi realized that the *shames* would leave and not return until the early morning. Upon investigation, he discovered that the *shames* went out to immerse himself in the freezing river and to cry for the destroyed Temple. With his secret revealed, Yosef Yozel left town.[6]

In time, Rav Yozel brought his family to Kovno and settled in Slobodka, a Kovno suburb. He studied Torah, standing on his feet for eighteen hours at a time. To fight off sleep, he had a special lectern made for his volumes, one that held the texts at eye level and forced him to frequently rise up on his toes. He absorbed knowledge and ideas from Rav Yitshak Blaser, with whom he had many long Musar conversations, and from Rav Avrohom Shenker, whose ways of ascetic piety he sought to emulate. He became well-known and was widely admired.

When Rav Yosef Yozel's father died, he was invited to assume the rabbinate of Kortobin. Instead he arranged a match for his sister with Rav Zelig Tarshish, who thus became the town's rabbi. Some of Rav Yosef Yozel's talmudic novellas from that period are quoted in Rav Zelig's work, *Ein Tarshish*. Rav Zelig went on to write many Torah works and became famous for his dedication to his community.

After bearing him a daughter and two sons, Rav Yozel's wife died in childbirth. He arranged for his children's care and removed himself to the house of a simple, poor Jew, Reb Shlomo Halevy, where he stayed for almost two years. The young scholar never left his dwelling, laboring incessantly and without distraction to advance in Torah

---

6. Rav Yisroel Salanter advised Rav Yosef Yozel to remain somewhat geographically distant from himself and his own overwhelming influence, so as to be able to develop independently.

and Fear of Heaven. His room was attached to the house from one side and enclosed by a courtyard fence on the other. There was no door or exit. No one could enter or leave the room except by breaking through the wall. In this manner he sought to avoid the entanglements and pitfalls of society.

He communicated with the outside world by means of a bell and, if he needed something, left messages by the window. The requested items were passed via two openings (one for meat and another for milk products) and an outside bell was then rung. Thus he was assured complete seclusion. A *mikva* was built into the enclosure and often Rav Yosef Yozel would immerse himself 310 times, in the fashion of the mystics. The future leader studied Torah and struggled to purify his soul. His study curriculum consisted primarily of the *Shulchan Aruch—Choshen Mishpat* and *Orach Chaim*, the works of the *Poskim* and Musar. Some of his Torah novellas from this time have been preserved. Often the passersby would hear faint cries of self-abnegation, or heartrending entreaties and prayers for knowledge and spiritual enlightenment.

This conduct provoked much attention. That the *Maskilim* used it to heap scorn upon the nascent Musar movement is not surprising; however, many prominent rabbis were also concerned. Rav Yitshak Blaser and Rav Yitzhak Elchonon Spector attempted to dissuade the hermit from his chosen path. On the other hand, there were many (among them, Reb Simcha Zissel Ziv) who said, "If a Jew wants to sit and labor in Torah and Musar, why should it bother anyone?"

An interesting exchange with Rav Yitzhak Elchonon Spector has been preserved. As the Rav of Kovno, he worried about the repercussions that such unusual behavior might bring from the *Maskilim* and the anti-Semitic and oppressive Czarist government. The Rabbi sent this message to the young recluse: "Why have you not come to the synagogue to hear the public blowing of the *shofar*?" Rav Yosef Yozel replied: "Does not the obligation to turn away from evil precede the one of doing good? The duty to escape the jealousy, and desires that come with the company of men takes precedence to that of hearing the *shofar* in public." The Rav of Kovno countered that it is possible to fulfill both obligations. "I have not yet reached that level," replied Rav Yosef Yozel.

The *Maskilim* were vexed by the attention that this example of dedication to a spiritual life attracted and by the beneficial effect it was beginning to have on the common folk. They conspired to plant counterfeit banknotes (some say revolutionary tracts) in the house and tip off the police. Thus they hoped to discredit and smear both Rav Yosef Yozel and the Kovno *Kollel*. On the day that the scheme was to be carried out, Rav Yosef Yozel's mother felt uneasy. It appeared to her that her son was in some kind of trouble, perhaps ill or indisposed. Despite her advanced age, she made the trip from Kortobin to see him. This was her first visit to her son in Kovno. He let her in and she found the counterfeit items in the antechamber. She quickly disposed of them. When the police barged in, they found nothing and angrily tore down the dwelling, forcing Rav Yosef Yozel to leave.

Although he was unable to sustain his isolation any longer, Rav Yosef Yozel continued to pursue his rigorous design for self-improvement. At this time, Reb Shlomo Halevy, the poor man who so generously allowed Rav Yosef Yozel to seclude himself in his house, finally succeeded in making a match for his daughter Chaya. Reb Shlomo Halevy was a poor man. Although he wished to marry Chaya to a scholar, many years passed without a suitable match. Finally he was able to arrange a fitting match and the wedding was set for after Sukkos. Before Rosh Hashana the groom broke the engagement; the pain of the distraught father and his abandoned daughter was plainly evident. Rav Yosef Yozel discovered this sad turn of events when he met his former benefactor on the street. The father's sorrow was obvious and the daughter's humiliation and pain were easily inferred. Rav Yosef Yozel was moved. On the spot, though after some reflection, he offered to marry Chaya. Reb Shlomo at first did not believe his good fortune. Rav Yosef Yozel insisted and they shook hands to bring the match to fruition. The young lady agreed, for she considered herself fortunate to marry a man of such high caliber.

The pressure to dissolve the match built up quickly and soon became intense. Rav Yosef Yozel was widely known for his scholarship and promise; he had rejected many prestigious matches.[7] Additionally, there was concern that marriage to the daughter of a former landlord might be utilized to cast aspersions upon the whole Musar movement. Rav Yosef Yozel did not yield and the marriage took place as planned.

Even after marriage, he continued upon his chosen path. He spent the week in seclusion, laboring in Torah and Musar. On *Shabbos* he joined his family but would speak only of Torah. During this period of his life, Rav Yosef Yozel spent time with well-known *Tzadikim*, such as Rav Leib of Stvisk, and further refined and developed his own Musar philosophy. He also founded several yeshivas, in a manner that foreshadowed his future approach. He would come to a town, gather the local youngsters, and speak to them about the greatness of Torah study. Once they agreed to join him, he would teach them, set up a functioning institution, and retain a well-known scholar to head it. Subsequently, he returned to seclusion and spent nine years in a forest dwelling built for him by Reb Gershon Tsirinsky from Zushen. His primary goal there was to learn how to trust God. He became known for ascetic ways. Many sought his advice regarding their own spiritual growth and visited him there. The Chofetz Chaim also sought him out at that time. Years later it was discovered that he had built a little hut even deeper in the forest where, unbeknownst to all, he spent long stretches of time. He made no provisions for food or any physical needs. There, he did not rely on man but on God's support alone. It always came through. In later years he often invoked his experiences from that forest hut when he spoke about trust in God.

Rav Yozel often traveled to Kelm to discuss Musar topics with Rav Simcha Zissel Ziv. The latter treated Rav Yosef Yozel with great respect, although he strongly disagreed with many of his views. Over the course of years, Rav Simcha Zissel was able to convince his friend

---

7. Some time earlier he traveled to Kelm upon advice of Rav Blaser to explore the possibilities of a match with Rav Simcha Zissel's daughter, Nechama Liba. This did not come to fruition.

to modify some of his opinions and to accept a role in the spreading of Musar. Rav Yosef Yozel continued to consider seclusion to be indispensable to self-improvement. He came to believe, however, that periods of separation can be incorporated into a spiritual lifestyle and combined with intense involvement with communal work. Throughout his later years, he continued to spend time alone, especially during periods of stress and opposition. This strengthened his resolve to proceed despite all odds and to push himself to greater efforts and exertion.

The courage and energy that were directed to self-conquest were now to be focused toward the wider world. Rav Yosef Yozel took over control of the fund set up by the noted philanthropist Ovadia Lachman in Kovno, under titular direction of Rav Yitshak Elchonon Spector and previously administered by Rav Yitshak Blaser. Rav Yitshak Blaser continued as the overall director of this fund until he was replaced by the opponents of Musar. In the course of but a few years, Rav Yosef Yozel founded a number of *kollelim* for married students in towns such as Shauli, Dvinsk, Minsk, Warsaw, Berditchev, Novarodok, Odessa, Lida, and Zetel.

These institutions trained future leaders of the Jewish people. Rav Yosef Yozel succeeded in imbuing his students with a longing for self-improvement and a desire to spread and strengthen Torah study. In these institutions, to be a *Rosh Yeshiva* was considered an ultimate goal and to teach Torah was more prestigious than to serve as a community rabbi. Even the graduates, who of necessity had accepted rabbinical positions, longed to set up small yeshivas in their towns. The number of such academies grew larger and larger and many of them were marked by a certain similarity of outlook. By 1886 it was evident that there was a need to create a central yeshiva where the graduates of these academies could pursue advanced studies.

# 2
# The Yeshiva in Novarodok

Rav Yosef Yozel was a capable organizer. A yeshiva was quickly set up and began to flourish in the town of Novarodok (Novogrudsk). The rabbi of the town, Rav Yechiel Michel Epstein, author of *Aruch Hashulchan*, lent his great prestige to the new institution. He provided letters of recommendation and his support rapidly enabled the new yeshiva to become well-known. There were those who criticized the venerable sage for supporting a Musar institution. To this, he replied, "I do not agree with all of the ways of Rav Yosef Yozel and, in fact, I myself complain about some of them. Yet when I enter the yeshiva and see his dedication and his awesome influence, all the accusations fade away." On another occasion he characterized Rav Yosef Yozel as "the unique one in this enterprise in our generation."[1]

---

1. He led the public defence of Musar against its detractors headed by Rav Zvi Hirsh Rabinovits, son of Rabbi Yitshak Elchonon of Kovno, and later by Rav Aharon Hacohen Burshtein (who briefly assumed the rabbinate of Novarodok after Rav Yechiel Michel Epshtein's passing). This phase of opposition to Musar appears to have been provoked to a great extent by the activities of Rav Yosef Yozel and the spread of his philosophy. Rav Burshtein became an antagonist of the Novarodok yeshiva after his move to Novarodok, although later in life he and Rav Yosef Yozel became reconciled. Cf. R. Meir Berlin's account, quoted in *Pulmus Hamusar*, p. 235 and p. 251, and Ch. 8.

Rav Yosef Yozel's family remained in Slobodka while he worked tirelessly for this academy. He returned home twice a year, for Sukkos and for Pesach holidays, and accepted only the barest necessities of life from the yeshiva. His wife supported herself and her children by selling pastries.

The yeshiva prospered and soon the enrollment reached three hundred students. There was also a sixty-member *kollel* for married scholars. The yeshiva was financed primarily by Reb Dov Zeldovitz, a magnate, a scholar, and a follower of Rav Yisroel Salanter.

This institution was unique in its approach to Torah study. In the beginning, Rav Yozel singlehandedly performed all of the customary functions. In addition to fundraising and administering the yeshiva, he delivered all the *shiurim*. To this end he spent some time with Rav Chaim Soloveitchik, in order to absorb the latter's talmudic style, which was then transforming the methods of Torah study. With the institution's expansion, Rav Yosef divided the students into *chavuros* (study groups), headed by the best products of the yeshiva. This novel arrangement demonstrated to each student that he also could achieve success and could advance in learning; it proved to be immensely salutary. Of course, the study of Musar was encouraged and gradually solidified into the form of what came to be called "Novarodoker Musar."

# 3
# *The Storming of the Soul*

Novarodok sought a complete restructuring of the self and believed that this could only be achieved through an emotional storm, through radical striving, and by great and noble deeds. This was an extension of the sentiment expressed by Rav Yisroel Salanter, who wrote: "The imagination is a raging stream and the mind will be submerged if one does not lead it in a boat—that is the striving of the soul and the storm of the spirit" (*Igeres Hamusar*). Rav Yosef Yozel developed this concept into a complete and remarkable set of teachings. He was deeply convinced that to awaken oneself, to find the unique keys that each person specifically requires, one must dedicate oneself totally and with no compromise. In our times one can no longer seek self-perfection by keeping to the golden mean. It is no longer possible to "walk the straight path" in the corrupt and devious world of today. One must rise above the world and even above oneself, above all personal and physical concerns. One must be *mafkir*, "give up oneself," and completely nullify one's self-interest, one's personhood, one's very essence. After all, a person falls short of greatness only because he wants something for himself. This varies with each individual. For a lowly person it may be some petty concern; for a great person, something more elevated. The self stands in the way of desiring only that which God commanded. The way to surmount this major barrier lies in learning how to sacrifice all that may be dear and precious in one's eyes, whatever the cost. A servant of God must totally restructure the core of his being; he must tear down the edifices of falsehood and vanity around himself and be rebuilt from scratch. Unlike students in other Musar yeshivas, many in Novarodok spent extended periods in Musar reflection, sometimes even at the expense of study. Still, the level of Torah learning remained very high and the movement produced many great scholars. The Musar of Novarodok was unique. It was said that one who did not personally experience the fire and the emotion of Novarodok could not conceive of true enthusiasm.

A person who entered the room set aside for Musar would be confronted with a remarkable sight. In one corner against the wall, there stands a young man. He cries out the words of *Shaarei Teshuva* (1,10) with all his might: "How did I exchange the world that persists forever for this passing world. Woe, I became likened unto an animal and followed my inclination like a horse, a mule without reckoning. And I erred from the way of knowledge. Why do I live?!" In another corner, a student rocks back and forth with a heartfelt refrain: "Envy, lust, and honor lead a man out of this world." This he repeats again and again with deep conviction and feeling. Another man paces back and forth with a mournful chant on his lips. A youngster sits in the corner with his head in his hands and weeps to God to give him "a pure heart to serve You, to serve You in truth."[1] Near pandemonium reigns. An atmosphere of somber reflection, exalted emotion, and spiritual striving pervades the room.

Rav Yosef Yozel did not accept the approach of Kelm that sought to uplift a person through gradual purification of the self, in the context of disciplined daily life and study. He felt that this approach deprived one of the reserves of feeling and emotion that are indispensable in the battle for self-mastery. Rage, emotion, and passion are the only tools that can break open the heart and the mind, empty it of all unworthiness and allow inner rebirth. In addition, he believed that

---

1. There were specific verses with the traditional assigned Novarodok chants that were often utilized for these sessions. Later, a number of songs with Yiddish lyrics and haunting melodies were specifically composed for this purpose.

such an approach did not allow sufficient space for individual development. Every person has his own unique task in life. To hold up one specific personality type as the desired goal can result in frustration and oftentimes can induce a man to pursue a shallow, insincere path. It leads people to acquire a superficial gloss of Musar accomplishments, while allowing them to avoid facing their true inner challenges (*Madreigas Ho'odom*, p. 139). Neither did he agree with the view of Slobodka that the proper goal is attainment of spiritual nobility through intense intellectual reflection. He was convinced that the soul must be jolted to be transformed and to withstand the trials of life, and that the goal of Musar study must be an awakening of ecstatic longing for the good and an equally powerful distaste for all that is petty and selfish. Then and only then can the intellect and the emotion fuse into a new personality.

As the other branches of the Musar movement matured, the original elements of the Musar approach became, at times, obscured by the wealth of insight and detail that its teachers discovered in the Talmud and the Midrash. For some, Musar became a theoretical philosophy, an approach to understanding man, the world, and society, rather than a practical science of living. Rav Yeruchom Levovits once commented: "The words of Rav Yisroel Salanter were all Musar. The teachings of Rav Simcha Zissel were a blend of Musar and wisdom. What we say is all words of wisdom."

In Novarodok, Musar remained supreme. The goal of Musar study was to transform the heart. Among the innovations of Novarodok was the *Musar Chavura* and the *Birzhe*, the most outstanding features of its unique approach. Students were encouraged to form minisocieties dedicated to a specific common spiritual goal. Unlike the case in other yeshivas, here the *chavura* functioned as a means to motivate its members and fan the flames of their enthusiasm. Rav Yozel believed that one cannot properly arouse oneself outside of a group. "The fire of many twigs is higher and stronger than the splattering of a single kindling. Together they will weed out crooked and unbecoming motivations and be able to extend the insights that each one needs." The members kept ledgers of their resolutions and actions. At each session a lot was cast and one member was selected to bare his soul. He would present a specific goal to which he aspired and of which he fell short. This might be his desire to overcome the craving for honor or his fervent wish to better appreciate Torah study or to achieve a more organized approach to overcoming impediments to ecstatic prayer. He had to verbalize self-criticism and had to list his strengths and the factors that interfered with further advancement. Finally, he had to accept specific resolutions and strategies to deal with these factors. The members of a *chavura* had no secrets from one another. Neither did they refrain from subjecting one another to scathing criticism. They called themselves the "searchers," the seekers for Truth. Many emotions and interpersonal entanglements can arise in groups of people who are this close. Rav Yozel wrote extensively about dealing with these challenges and about how to make them springboards for further advancement (*Madreigas Ho'odom*, p. 210–213).

Rav Yozel adopted the *birzhe* method from the revolutionaries who favored group meetings, in which matters of Marxist doctrine were hotly debated. These gatherings tended to be noisy, free-for-all affairs that inevitably split into animated, intense, and fluid discussions between small groups and individuals. Rav Yosef Yozel himself frequently participated in these discussions. The name *birzhe* was selected because these gatherings, in their excitement, resembled the stock exchange, the bourse. Rav Yosef Yozel would say "They do their thing and we do ours. They evaluate the rise and fall of stocks and we measure the rise and descent of the soul." The *birzhe* took place outside of the usual study hours, twice a week during the year and daily in *Elul*. Younger students were paired with seasoned veterans and the debates would begin. No holds were barred and all of life's questions were on the agenda. No one was immune to penetrating probing and examination of his habits, beliefs, and patterns of behavior. Various approaches to spiritual dilemmas were considered and accepted, discarded, or referred to others for evaluation. There was no "true" answer. The goal of these exercises was to purify the soul and teach the habits of critical self-examination, to prepare for a life of Musar and striving. The power of this method of Musar study lay in its ability to set free the thinking process in an informal setting and to bring together emotional and intellectual arousal. The participants paced back and forth while thus occupied. This further enlivened and animated the discussion. Often, even those students whose dedication to the life of spirit was more apparent than real, were drawn into the fray and changed by the experience. Through the *birzhe*, new arrivals were quickly initiated into the spirit of Novarodok. Many learned the art of public speaking and debate in these exchanges, a skill that enabled them to spread the teachings of their master in the years to come.

In Novarodok there was no private property. All that one had, whether clothing, personal items, or books, was available to all. The owner of a new coat was expected to lend it to others before wearing it himself, to remove the taint of possessiveness from his heart. Spiritual fortitude was combined with disregard for comfort and material things. Rav Yosef Yozel often quoted *Sanhedrin* 20a: "'The woman who fears God, she shall be praised' (Proverbs 31:30)—This is the generation of Rabbi Yehudah ben Ilai. It was said that six students would wear a single cloak and be occupied in Torah."

"It is clear," he would say, "that Fear of Heaven and lack of means are interrelated."

Every month of the year was dedicated to the practice of a specific character trait. During *Nisan* they practiced seclusion. Whereas in other yeshivas these days ushered in general relaxation, in anticipation of Passover holidays and the summer break, in Novarodok unique events would take place. Groups of students headed by leaders of their *chavuras* fanned out into the surrounding countryside. They took up residence in the synagogues and Houses of Study in local towns and villages, to be supported by their inhabitants. They studied Talmud and Musar with great enthusiasm. Many also refrained from speaking of non-Torah subjects—the so called *Taanis Dibur*, a "verbal fast."

In *Iyar* they worked on removing the desire for honor, in *Tamuz* on improving the purity of motivation. When new students arrived in *Cheshvan*, it was time to practice benevolence to others, and in *Teves* to train themselves in aspiring to greatness and austerity. Around Chanuka was the time for practicing complete and total reliance on

God. Students would get a one-way ticket to a distant destination with not a penny in their pockets. From there they endeavored to make their way back without asking anyone for help. Gaunt, pale, silent men that never asked for assistance were a common sight in Lithuanian towns and villages and kindhearted householders knew enough to offer them food and lodgings. Before Purim they practiced boldness of spirit and disregard for ridicule for "Mordechai did not rise nor tremble" (Esther 5:9). A student would repeatedly go to a hardware store and ask for flour or to a grocery and ask for nails. Some entered strangers' homes on the *Shabbos* afternoon and asked for bread for their third Sabbath meal, for this was described in the Musar work, *Yesod Hatshuva*, as an act of courage. Some students paraded down the city streets in muddy and tattered clothing. In this fashion they trained themselves not to fear ridicule. Some Novarodokers generally wore poorly fitting apparel and at times made public spectacles of themselves, in order to teach themselves the inner fortitude and courage to stand in opposition to the whole world, if necessary, and to pursue their goals without flinching.

The month of *Elul* was special in Novarodok. The students from many other schools came to town during this time period to imbibe the rarefied atmosphere that reigned there. The emphasis was on repentance and inner rebirth. Musar became the predominant subject of study during this period. The prayers were especially long and heartfelt and souls stirred and moved with spiritual fervor. Frequent gatherings were held, during which "words of awakening" were spoken—to enflame the souls and hearts and to move the audience to repentance. Many of the boys spent extended periods in reflection, preparing themselves for confrontation with their deepest faults, and then sought out the places and situations where they had previously failed—this time to conquer and to win. Regret for the past and longing for purity pervaded the yeshiva.

Correspondingly, the Succos holidays that followed the season of repentance were exhilarating, "the time of our joy." Every person felt he had become a new being and rejoiced without restraint.

The hands-on approach to practicing and living Musar had an immediate effect on its practitioners. Rav Chaim Boruch Faskowitz relates: "One cold winter day, a group of us, all young boys of thirteen to fourteen years old, had to get to the other side of town. It was snowing but this was close to Chanuka, a time to practice *Bitachon*. We decided that we will go by bus. Now, this was already in Bialistok. The Polish bus drivers were notorious anti-Semites. They often threw even paying Jewish passengers off their buses, and we had no money. Still, we were determined to travel only thus. We stood and waited in heavy snow. Several times Jewish textile transporters stopped their horse-driven buggies and offered us a free ride but we refused. Suddenly, a bus pulled up in front of us. The Polish driver invited us to enter and agreed to drive us to our destination without pay. That experience taught me more about *Bitachon* than all the Musar lectures in the world."

Novarodok was intensely personal and deeply emotional. The goal was to wrench the soul from its moorings; in this, every student was his own teacher. Each man was responsible for himself and his neighbor and for all of Jewry. In Novarodok, Musar was not an abstraction or an interesting set of teachings; it was a very direct and intense personal struggle with very specific and intimate goals.[2]

A prominent rabbi once asked Rav Yozel: "Isn't this way more suited for the preceding generations than for us now? How can you expect that thousands of students can master such a demanding and diffi-

---

2. It is of interest to note that, for his students, Rav Yosef Yozel did not stress separation from society and self-seclusion of the kind that he himself found so useful in his youth and continued to utilize as part of his own spiritual practices throughout life. It may be that he considered his own experience binding only on himself because of his own individual and unique spiritual makeup. He may have felt that seclusion was necessary to develop the philosophy of Novarodok but was no longer needed once this was accomplished. Now, study of Musar in a group is most effective. Alternatively, he may have felt that this method is so powerful and so fraught with the danger of spiritual injury that it cannot be routinely recommended to the masses of his followers or to his many young and still inexperienced students.

cult discipline?" He answered with an analogy: "This is like a carpentry shop. Huge trees are cut into boards to produce all kinds of items. From these boards they make exquisite planks for ornate Holy Arks, as well as other, plainer items. One also ends up with shavings and sawdust that are used for many vital purposes. Does anyone think, however, that the purpose of the shop is to produce shavings? Of course not. The goal is to produce commodities, not by-products. Similarly, our purpose is to produce men of distinction—scholars and luminaries. The remainder also have great value. Every Jew is as precious as gold. Still, let each student worry whether he has reached the heights of his colleague, for "the jealousy of scribes increases wisdom" (*Bava Basra* 21a).

In 1917 Rav Yitzhak Elchonon Valdshein began to transcribe notes of Rav Yosef Yozel's talks. These were reviewed and edited by Rav Yosef Yozel prior to publication. Over the subsequent years, he circulated twelve booklets among the students. The first edition of the work was published in Poltava and the subsequent sections were brought out in Pietrikov several years later. These were put together and published in New York in 1949, under the name *Madreigas Ho'odom* (The Level of Man).

## 4
## The Years of Trouble

Although the unfolding of Rav Yosef Yozel's Musar philosophy was gradual, a major impetus for its development were the events of the failed Russian revolution of 1905. Its universalist slogans and promises of liberation from the oppressive Czarist yoke, which lay heavily on the impoverished Jewish masses, succeeded in enticing some yeshiva students to join various revolutionary movements and groups. A specific occurrence was particularly poignant and led Rav Yozel to intensify the study of Musar in his school.

A student from the town of Simiatits was known for his dedication to Torah study. He appeared to have no other interests and his diligence was phenomenal. During a visit to his parents, however, he underwent a sudden transformation. Upon his return, he appeared to have lost all enthusiasm for study and soon left to join the communists.

To Rav Yosef Yozel, this episode demonstrated that in these turbulent times Torah study alone was no longer sufficient to assure spiritual progress. Only through intensive Musar study could the tide be turned.

After Rav Yechiel Michel Epstein passed away, another yeshiva was founded in Novarodok. This school was led and supported by the new rabbi, Rav Menachem Korkovsky, who was not among the supporters of Musar. The new institution did not favor the existence of a Musar academy in town and relations between the two academies became strained. During World War I, the newer yeshiva was dissolved. Rav Yosef Yozel, on the other hand, refused to close his school. Instead, he advertised his readiness to admit students of any other yeshiva closed by the war. In the crucible of war and deprivation the students of Novarodok strived for greatness.

Rav Yehuda Leib Nekrits, later a leader of the movement in Brooklyn, compared Rav Yosef Yozel to a meteor that flashed over the frozen Siberian tundra. For thousands of years the ground lay covered by ice and snow that hid untold mineral wealth. The flaming visitor from space thawed these out and exposed fabulous riches for all to see. The Jewish nation also lay fallow and untended, under the cover of indifference and habit. The masses hungered for relief from their grinding poverty and oppression and they sought deliverance in materialistic philosophies and pursuits. Rav Yosef Yozel revealed the greatness that is within every Jew, for he set aflame the hearts of his many students and inspired them to seek spiritual grandeur.

Soon after the outbreak of hostilities, western Poland and Lithuania (then a part of Russia) became a battleground. Although the German army was better disposed to the Jews than the undisciplined and deeply anti-Semitic Russian forces were, Rav Yosef Yozel, utilizing the *goral Hagro*[1] decided to move the yeshiva deeper into Russia. He knew that Judaism was greatly compromised in the German-speaking lands; concern for a proper environment for Torah study was uppermost in his mind. In addition, the Russian interior was full of dispossessed Jewish refugees from Lithuania and Poland. Raf Yozel felt a sense of responsibility to provide them with spiritual support. He traveled to Belarus and the Ukraine to scout out a new place for the yeshiva and found the requisite circumstances in Gomel. During this brief period, the Germans advanced on Novarodok. The students followed their teacher and fled to the Ukraine. By foot, carriage, and train, amidst

---

1. A method of deciding on a course of action guided by a biblical verse. For a description of the traditional method see *A Tzadik in Our Times* by Simcha Raz (Feldheim, 1977), pp. 165–168.

the masses of fleeing refugees they braved hunger, marauders, disease, and uncertainty.

The yeshiva was reestablished in Gomel in 1914 with about eighty students. Those who made their way to Gomel were the most dedicated and committed, the best products of the yeshiva. The chaos that surrounded them did not cool their ardor. It was precisely during those arduous times that the yeshiva reached the pinnacle of spirituality. The students did not pay heed to their physical needs. Often there was no food and no fuel. They wore tattered clothing and went hungry, but they set the yeshiva aflame with their desire for more Divine Service, for greater and greater advancement, for more and more spiritual growth. Rav Yosef Yozel was at the peak of his powers. He seemed to have divested himself of his physical being and had no need for food, clothing, or shelter. His only goal was to achieve greater heights in the service of God and to reach others with his message. Precisely in those difficult times, when all organized Torah study was in danger of disappearing, he saw the opportunity to demonstrate that *Musar* can overcome all obstacles. He did not draw back when other yeshivas disbanded but actively recruited the many lost and wandering students of these schools for his yeshiva.

Gomel was at that time a major railroad hub and many of the displaced students from Radun, Mir, Slobodka, and other yeshivas passed through town. Every day the students of Novarodok spread through the city looking for their lost brethren. This often required great courage and self sacrifice. They succeeded. The yeshiva grew and soon its students numbered in the hundreds.

Not only the learned were welcomed. Rav Yosef Yozel also searched out the boys who had never studied Torah or those who did not come from observant homes. There was often strong opposition and even danger from physical harm in these forays. On one occasion, Rav Yozel entered the local secular school and delivered a heartfelt and moving address on the greatness of Torah study. Many of the students who heard him were influenced to set up Torah study circles in town and some eventually joined his yeshiva.

The war went on and soon all young men were made subject to the draft. The students of the yeshiva disregarded their conscription notices. This was a capital offense in the time of war but, miraculously, not one of them was ever harmed. Occasionally, pupils were picked up in massive street sweeps conducted by the government to catch "deserters" but somehow they were always able to escape. The searches, however, were becoming more frequent and Rav Yosef Yozel decided to spread his boys throughout the towns of Russia and the Ukraine. There, farther from the front, the police pressure was less intense; more importantly, there were many Jewish refugees adrift in the vast expanses of the country. The students were to reestablish centers of Torah among these exiles and counter their spiritual drift away from observance and Torah learning. Rav Yozel was aided in this undertaking by Rav Chaim Ozer Grodzinski, who was then in Gomel. Each senior student was assigned a group of younger boys and was sent to a town. They moved into the local synagogues and, whether welcome or not, whether financially supported or not, they took root and flourished. Sometimes they had to overcome strong opposition; usually little material support was available. The youngsters succeeded against all odds and established major yeshivas in Kiev, Charkov, Nizhni-Novgorod, Rostov, Tsaritsin (Volgagrad), Saratov, Pavlograd, and Tchernigov. A yeshiva was even established in the shadow of the Kremlin in Moscow but it did not survive. Each of these centers was surrounded by a network of elementary and grammar schools under the supervision of the mother institution. The schools were generally set up to consist of three parts. At the core of each yeshiva was a group of students who dedicated themselves to study of the Talmud, with the commentaries of Rashi and Tosefos. On the second level were those who were more advanced; they attended a traditional *shiur*. Another group of advanced scholars studied independently. Two older members of this group were put in charge of running the yeshiva and supervising its material and spiritual well-being.

A number of established yeshivas were "captured" by the Novarodokers, often with the assistance of Rav Yosef Yozel himself. The students would move en masse into such a school and imbue it with the zeal and dedication of Novarodok. At times they were officially invited to uplift the spirit of an yeshiva and to counter the influence of the *Haskalah*. Such was the case in Slutsk, where Rav Yozel and a number of his students were invited by Rav Isser Zalman Meltser, the Rav of Slutsk. Rav Yozel spent several months with Rav Isser Zalman and instituted many of the Novarodok methods there. Slutsk became the only non-Novarodok institution where practical Musar techniques were utilized.

Each of these schools had a profound influence on its community. At the beginning of each school year, students spread throughout the surrounding countryside to speak to children on the streets and in the fields. They gathered the children and set up *chedorim* and elementary schools. Intense local opposition often arose to such activities but the Novarodokers were not easily deflected. Many of the children that they recruited later became great scholars and leaders of the next generation.

All of these schools remained in constant contact with Rav Yosef Yozel and his son-in-law Rav Avrohom Jofen, who served as the dean of the Gomel institution. During designated periods, Rav Yosef Yozel would visit each of the outlying academies and provide his personal guidance and influence. In addition, yearly gatherings of all Novarodok leaders were held and outstanding issues were discussed and resolved. Rav Yeruchom Liebovits, a great Musar personality, compared Rav Yosef Yozel to a cantor with a choir. "The choir assists the cantor and enriches his melodies. The other Musar leaders of the time can be compared to a cantor without a choir because their influence depends solely on their individual efforts."

# 5
# The Revolution

In 1917, the Bolsheviks overthrew the provisional democratic government and seized power. The great teeming masses of the Russian empire were set free from any authority as the Red Army battled the Whites and numerous local factions and militias fought each other. Murderous bands of demobilized soldiers and ruffians roamed the countryside, especially targeting Jews and merchants. Hundreds of thousands of Jews were murdered. There was no order and no government and human life was cheap. Famine and typhoid and cholera epidemics ranged unchecked and roads and railroad stations were choked with the refugees and the dispossessed. As the Communists took power, "class enemies" were mercilessly eliminated or exiled.

Novarodok was not afraid. With heroic disregard for personal safety, the students continued their activities. They cared not for borders or decrees. They moved from place to place to spread Torah and Musar. The boys infiltrated behind front lines to carry messages between yeshivas. Students fearlessly took the pulpit during Communist rallies and preached spiritual renewal. At times, they appeared in groups at show trials of the Jewish religion and made public demonstrations of their faith. They argued with the "prosecutors" and broke into Musar chants in the midst of the proceedings. They jostled soldiers and speculators for space on the roofs of overcrowded train cars and braved epidemics to carry out their assigned tasks. Contact and communication between academies was not broken and the movement remained united. On a number of occasions, these boys were suspected of being counterrevolutionaries or spies (a crime punishable by death) and were imprisoned. Some were pressed into forced labor and several succumbed to contagious illnesses. Still they did not desist.

Rav Yosef Yozel himself did the same. On Rosh Hashana he might be in Kiev, before Yom Kippur in Charkov, and on Yom Kippur in Gomel. Almost every *Shabbos* was spent in another place. Despite being over seventy years old, he jumped onto the roofs of passing trains and pushed himself in between cattle cars. During one such occasion, he spent several hours hanging from a metal cable that connects railcars, in the middle of the Russian winter. When he arrived at his destination, his hand was frozen to the metal. He was forced to leave skin and flesh behind in order to disembark. Rav Yozel's shining personality endeared him to his fellow travelers, the Russian peasants and soldiers, who often aided and assisted him. Amazingly, the annual gatherings continued despite all obstacles. As Communist control solidified, however, personal communication became impossible. The yeshivas exchanged coded telegraph messages, based on biblical verses and statements of the Sages. Once, for example, Rav Yosef Yozel received a telegram from Saratov. The Soviet government decreed that the local yeshiva must be closed. He wired these two words in response: "Av Harachamim." This is the title of a well-known Sabbath prayer dealing with martyrdom; it indicated that they must be prepared to give up their lives for their faith in the manner described in that prayer. When the commissar and the soldiers came to close the yeshiva, the dean refused to obey. The official then pointed a loaded rifle at him. The *Rosh Yeshiva* opened his shirt and cried out: "I am not afraid, shoot." Immediately, every student of the yeshiva lined up behind their teacher and did the same. Faced with this unexpected defiance, the Communists backed down and the yeshiva remained open.

Gradually the Bolsheviks solidified their power and began to extend ideological control over the population. The religious institutions were a thorn in their side. The Yevsektsia agents were especially viperous in their persecutions. Yevsektsia was the branch of the Communist secret police assigned the task of uprooting Jewish religion and communal life. It was staffed by renegade Jews whose hatred for rabbis and religious functionaries far surpassed the zeal of their non-Jewish counterparts in the other sections of the "Ministry for Religion."[1] These apostates persecuted Judaism without mercy and were devoid of any trace of sympathy or identification with their brethren. The rabbis who refused to cooperate were shot, imprisoned, or exiled to Siberia. In many places, "red" rabbis were imposed on the communities and in their synagogues they preached atheism and Communism under the portraits of Lenin and Marx. Religious books and objects derisively called "objects of cult" were confiscated. The situation deteriorated to such an extent that the students of Novarodok would gather together before every Rosh Chodesh to pronounce a blessing on an unquestionably kosher pair of *tefillin*, for many of them did not have a pair of their own or possessed *tefillin* of uncertain validity. The study of Torah before the age of eighteen was prohibited and its teachers were arrested and summarily executed. The masses were demoralized by incessant antireligious propaganda and economic pressure. "Voluntary" public works on the Sabbath were required throughout the country and public observance of religion became impossible. Sadly, to some degree these measures succeeded because of popular support. The people were worn out by war and deprivation and longed for relief at any price. Even many of the observant were demoralized and inwardly hoped that the Communist promise of a workers' paradise on earth would somehow soon materialize. The reverse side of this promise was that "he who does not work, does not eat." There was, therefore, precious little support for the "parasitic" yeshiva students on the Jewish street. It was clear that organized opposition was no longer viable in such circumstances and the yeshivas flowed to the Ukraine and Belarus, where Communists had triumphed only recently and where their hold was still somewhat tenuous. However, the situation deteriorated quickly there as well. Public trials of religion became

---

1. The methods of Yevsektsia are well described in *The Jewish Religion in the Soviet Union* by J. Rottenberg (New York: Ktav, 1971).

frequent; the students of Novarodok were often summoned and accused in these propaganda performances. Although they defended their faith with remarkable courage and conviction, the verdict was predetermined and often led to further persecution or even execution and exile. In the early years, petitions from "Jewish Proletarians" sometimes obtained temporary relief from incessant pressure or managed to salvage buildings in which the yeshivas found refuge. Later, such expressions of support were ignored or savagely suppressed.

In 1918 Rav Yosef Yozel moved the center of the movement to Kiev. The countryside was full of roaming bands from the disintegrating forces of Petlura, the Greens, and the forces of General Denikin, the Whites. Jews were beaten and killed and travel was impossible. The Novarodokers continued to study—in basements, in cemeteries, in the forests. Many were caught and imprisoned but, in a miraculous fashion, all managed to escape. The situation went from bad to worse. Waves of pogroms rolled through the country and tens of thousands were killed. Those who escaped found temporary refuge in Kiev. The city's synagogues and study halls were filled with refugees. To make matters worse, the forces of Denikin briefly captured the city and promptly carried out a major pogrom. Rav Yosef Yozel was then a father to three hundred students. He spread them equally throughout the city (five sections in town, plus two in the suburbs) and charged them to strengthen their brothers in their hour of need. He inspired them to trust God's mercies and to show their love and awe of Him through mighty deeds. In his Yom Kippur sermon, he quoted Nakdimon ben Gurion's prayer: "Master of the World, make it known that you have those whom you love in your World" (*Taanis* 20b). He told them that they must battle for truth and remain trustworthy, even unto death.

Before Succos the forces of Denikin that were briefly driven off again captured the city. This was followed by weeks of slaughter and violence. The carnage intensified and, by Simchas Torah, the streets were covered with bodies and echoed with gunfire and the wild screams of exultant murderers. Hundreds of Jews trusted in Rav Yosef's merit and sought refuge with him. On Simchas Torah morning, he ordered them to begin the *Hakafos*. To spare the fearful refugees, he told his students to dance in their stockings and to keep their voices down. He himself joined the procession with great joy, paying no regard to the violence outside. Still, the singing was heard in the street and the murderers entered the antechamber. Miraculously, they were apparently frightened off and retreated after firing several shots into the building.

After the holidays a typhoid epidemic spread through the city and took fifteen thousand lives in three months. The crowded Jewish quarters were especially hard hit. Only Rav Yosef Yozel and three students did not fall ill. Rav Yosef cared personally for the sick. He would say "I am not a greater *Yachsan* (a person of distinguished lineage) than anyone else." A woman in the neighborhood supplied food to the ailing students. She wanted to help wash the floors where the sick lay, but Rav Yosef Yozel refused her. He said that there was danger of catching the illness; therefore she was exempt. "But what about you?" she asked. "I am already an old man," he replied. She thought he had refused her because of religiously inspired concerns about modesty, so she volunteered her husband. Rav Yozel gently explained to her that in Novarodok one does not entrust the care of the sick to others for they may not expend adequate effort in performing this holy task (*Tosefos Yoma* 84b). Faithfully, he continued to care for the sick until he fell ill himself. Even with a high fever, he aroused himself from his sickbed to take care of others. Rav Yozel continued to encourage his students and to speak to them of Musar and fear of Heaven. His illness worsened and, on the night of the seventeenth of *Kislev* of 5680 (1920), his holy spirit returned to its Maker.

Despite the danger, thousands gathered for his funeral. All of the city's rabbis eulogized this remarkable man. Rav Dovid Budnik, one of Rav Yosef Yozel's closest disciples, was the last speaker. He had been in bed with a high fever but arose to pay his last respects to his great teacher. His heartfelt words rang in the ears of the crowd—"He did not die; he lives in us." Right then and there, they all accepted the following resolution: "We will not turn from his inheritance or ever leave his exalted path. To serve with all that remains of our strength, with great fortitude, and stand like a rock in the heart of the seas to support the existing yeshivas and to found new ones, greater in numbers and quality, so that they will not ever move [from their foundation]. To carry the flag of Torah and fear of God in splendor and might throughout Jewry for all of our days."

# 6
# The Next Generation

The movement continued to thrive. New yeshivas were established in the areas recently captured by the Red Army. Rav Avrohom Jofen was then in Gomel, which was controlled by the Reds. The front lines separated him from Kiev. Somehow, the news of his teacher's passing reached him. Clearly, his place was in Kiev but how could one cross the lines of fire? Novarodok provided the answer: one must fear no man. The thirty-three-year-old scholar sought out Lev Trotsky, who was directing the war effort from Gomel. "I must get to Kiev to comfort the persecuted Jewish masses," he told the commander of the Red Army. Trotsky was a cunning, brilliant leader and a complicated personality. His word was law and he was capable of unspeakable cruelties. He allowed his own father to starve to death for being a member of the capitalist class. One gesture from him could send thousands to their graves. Yet Trotsky was moved by this appeal and extended his assistance. Rav Jofen was escorted to the front lines and smuggled across by Soviet agents. From Kiev he led the movement and was assisted by Rav Dovid Budnik in his yeshiva in Zhitomir. A central conference was held in Gomel a year and a half after Rav Yosef Yozel's passing and it was resolved that his methods and goals be perpetuated.

Rav Jofen labored to persevere in his activities despite all difficulties. Unfortunately, as the Communists tightened their grasp, the persecutions became unbearable. Many of the students were arrested and, in 1921, Rav Jofen himself was imprisoned. The immediate impetus that led to his arrest was the intervention of a high-ranking Jewish commissar. His son had run away to join the Gomel yeshiva without his father's knowledge. When the father discovered this, he had his son forcibly removed and brought home. A delegation from Gomel clandestinely traveled to the young man's town and spirited him away, back to the yeshiva. The commissar was furious and called in his connections. Rav Jofen and several senior students were arrested on charges of counterrevolutionary activities and were threatened with the death penalty. Rav Jofen underwent merciless interrogation, several details of which have been preserved. It is said that the jailers were most interested in discovering the nature of methods by which he was able to secure such loyalty and dedication. "If I only had two hundred followers like yours," the chief interrogator told Rav Jofen," I could conquer the whole world." At another time, he told the prisoner that Moses was a revolutionary who led the oppressed masses in an uprising against Pharaoh. "We also are like him," he argued. "You must join us." Rav Jofen replied, "Moses was not a revolutionary at all. The proof of that is that he died peacefully forty years later, in his allotted time." The truth of this insight was borne out sixteen years later, when Stalin carried out purges that eliminated the "old" Communist guard.

Among those who were imprisoned was the future Torah giant, Rabbi Yakov Kanievsky (the Steipler), who later served as *Rosh Yeshiva* of the Novarodok branch in Pinsk. In the "bear's den," Torah study went on. But how could religious books be brought into a Communist prison? A solution was not far off. Pages of the Talmud were wrapped around bread and fish and were smuggled into jail, enabling the schedule of studies to go on. This ingenious method of contraband was approved by the famed Rav of Minsk, who said: "As I see it, we are dealing with a situation of mortal danger. To leave followers of Novarodok without Torah is *Pikuach Nefesh*. So, one can even expose the holy books to some degree of disrespect" (possibly based on the Rambam, *Rotseach*, 7:1). Due to intense international pressure, Rav Jofen was eventually released and a trial date was set. The others were punished with several months of hard labor.

For two years an unequal struggle raged between a small band of impoverished students, armed only with their convictions, and the newly established Soviet power, with all the resources of the modern police state. At times, it appeared that Novarodok might actually be gaining; the numbers of students grew to a total of six hundred. By 1922, however, it became clear that organized resistance could no longer be sustained. Following the advice of the Chofets Chaim, the decision was made to move the yeshivas to Poland.

Many of the students were Polish citizens and were eligible for repatriation. Others claimed Polish descent in order to escape the country. The boys left behind their loved ones and their homes, knowing that they would never see them again. Some of them were not yet thirteen years old. They were not even able to say good-bye to their families because of the secrecy that was required. For almost a year and a half, in small groups, hungry, barefoot, and in tattered clothes, they smuggled themselves across borders, to be welcomed by Jews of nearby towns. They walked in darkness across fields and forests, covering miles of dangerous and inhospitable terrain. This was not a simple undertaking and many were caught by the Communists and apprehended. When asked for passports, they presented a copy of *Chovos Halevovos*. We know of at least one occasion when this ruse worked. The illiterate guards were impressed by the thick binding and ornate cover of this "passport" and let them through. Others escaped and tried again, repeating the process many times. The Steipler, for example, was left alone with a peasant woman guide when the others heard the whistles of the Soviet border police and scattered in all directions. Rather than risk transgressing the prohibition of being secluded alone with a woman, the Steipler turned back into Russia. He subsequently crossed with another group. Often the students lost all they had to brigands and had to return empty-handed. Many were arrested by the Poles and were led in chains to their towns, to be released upon positive identification by their families. The students from Gomel were the last to cross.

The first yeshiva in Poland was founded by Rav Jofen in Bialistok. With three hundred and twenty students, it quickly became the spiritual center of the Novarodok movement. Other schools were established in Mezritch, Warsaw, Simiatits, Pinsk, and Latvia. These schools were named "Beis Yosef" in memory of their great teacher. The name also recalls the verse by the prophet Ovadia: ". . . and the house of Yosef shall be a flame" (*Ovadia* 1,18). The yeshivas really did spread like wildfire. Over the ensuing years, each one became a magnet around which smaller academies were organized. At the final count, more than ninety yeshivas, with three to four thousand students, thrived in Poland under the name Beis Yosef. The Bialistok yeshiva was at the center of thirty institutions in the surrounding towns and villages. The group of schools administered from Mezritch consisted of twenty-three yeshivas. The Warsaw branch managed eleven schools. The Pinsk yeshiva oversaw fifteen and the Beis Yosef in Dvinsk was responsible for a network of six institutions. The center of the movement was in Bialistok, while Rav Dovid Bliacher led a branch in Mezritch. The group in Warsaw was under the leadership of Rav Avrohom Zalmanes. Rav Shmuel Veintrob and the Steipler led the yeshiva in Pinsk and Rav Dovid Budnick headed the yeshiva in Dvinsk. A network of schools was developed in Riga by Rav Yoel Baranchik. Each central institution educated several hundred students, in addition to those in its branches. In 1929 Rav Jofen visited the land of Israel, where he helped Rav Hillel Vitkind start a branch in Tel Aviv. That same year, a seed was planted in England when a Novarodok yeshiva was set up in Gateshead. This eventually developed into a major complex of world-renowned Torah institutions. In 1932 another Beis Yosef was opened in Bnei Brak. The Chazon Ish delivered lectures in this yeshiva, until his brother-in-law, the Steipler, arrived from Poland and assumed the post of the *Rosh Yeshiva*.

# 7
# The House of Joseph in Poland

The challenges that Novarodok faced in its new country were quite different from the trials that it underwent in Russia. A new generation had to be drawn to its teachings, a generation that grew up in the relative tranquility of postwar Poland. The chasidic world that dominated Polish orthodoxy was secure in its own way of serving God. The Enlightenment had spent itself, attempting to present a serious challenge to religion; now its sons were ready to be swept back into the luster of Lithuanian Torah learning. Polish Jewry was ready for a revolution, but a revolution carried out slowly and deliberately, by teaching and by example. Rav Avrohom Jofen followed faithfully in his teacher's footsteps. He never ceased to consider himself merely a disciple of Rav Yosef Yozel (in fact, he called his talmudic commentaries *Derech Aisan*, which stands for Avrohom Jofen, *Talmid* Novarodok). Yet now his task was to situate the movement as an integral part of the yeshiva world, to clarify its traditions and establish its texts and customs. He used to say: "When a caravan crosses dry land, there is no choice but to follow the leading wagon. When far away at sea, however, the captain must rely only on his compass and his instruments. It is not possible just to follow someone else." Rav Jofen's scholarship earned him and his yeshiva their rightful place among the spiritual aristocracy of Jewish Poland. One could no longer dismiss Novarodok as a small group of eccentrics, for its high level of scholarship and the stature of its *Rosh Yeshiva* spoke for themselves. Important works of scholarship were published by students of Novarodok, amongst them *Shaarei Tvuna*, written by the Steipler, as well as collections of *Musar* articles, and thoughts in the form of notes and periodicals.

Rav Jofen delivered two *shiurim* each week. He would focus on the views of the *Rishonim* and then explicate the *sugya* according to the views of later commentaries. During his lecture, he pointed out difficulties and contradictions. At his conclusion, he would posit a lucid analysis or a novel proposition that resolved these problems in a most wondrous manner. These lectures were very highly regarded and were often copied and disseminated in other yeshivas. On Friday night, after the conclusion of the *Shabbos* and once during the week, he delivered Musar talks. These focused on the riches hidden in the weekly Torah reading and on the midrashic passages that related to it. Invariably, he concluded with the exhortation: "And if this is how things are, there can be no greater thing than the study of Musar and, especially, to study with enthusiasm." Rav Jofen considered informal discussions on Musar topics to be of utmost importance. He therefore insisted that such discussions follow his talks.

The Musar element continued to imbue Novarodok yeshivas with a unique atmosphere and character. Many students, who may have considered the study of *Musar* to be incidental, came because of the high level of Torah study. Nevertheless, they also absorbed the unique flavor of reflection and striving that characterized Novarodok. Rav Chaim Shmulevitz, the noted *Rosh Yeshiva* of Mir, said:

> I was fortunate to dwell in those days in the shadow of our great master, Rav Shimon Shkop, in the yeshiva of Grodno. There was no greater teacher of Torah anywhere. I was especially fortunate that I was able to also deliver daily lectures in his yeshiva. But despite all this, despite the fact that no man could ever have been more fortunate, from time to time, a certain "coldness" enveloped me. When one feels "cold," he

must "warm up." There is but one place for this. Where? In a Novarodok yeshiva. I would take a train to Bialistok and refresh my soul.

Every morning the students walked to a local house of study (not part of the yeshiva) to study Musar. This was not officially part of the study schedule but it was understood to be highly recommended. Some studied for a few minutes, some for half an hour, a few longer. Rav Avrohom Jofen then appeared for his own Musar study period. He paced back and forth, chanting with great enthusiasm from *Chovos Halevovos* until his face shined with spiritual pleasure, as befitted one who was partaking of otherworldly delights.

The Musar *chavuros* were well-organized and each student belonged to a group that was appropriate for his level. The highest, named "Generals," was an elite group that included the Steipler, Rav Elchonon Valdshein, and Rav Aharon Ogolnik. All of this group's members became leaders in their own right in subsequent years. "The Tenth is Holy" was composed of the second tier of scholars. Rav Nissan Bobroisker belonged to this select group. Rav Chaim Zaitchik belonged to the next group—"The Seekers." The next *chavura* was made up of those who came from Russia, including Rav Yehuda Leib Nekrits, the future son-in-law of Rav Jofen and the *Rosh Yeshiva* in the Beis Yosef in Brooklyn. Rav Gershon Liebman, the founder of the Ohr Yosef network in France, was also a member of this illustrious fellowship. Rav Ben-Tsion Bruk, future leader of the movement in Israel, led one of several groups designed for the Polish-born students.

At the head of each *chavura* stood a student who himself belonged to one of the more advanced groups. He was assisted by a student from one of the intermediate levels. A meeting was held weekly. At that time, a program of Musar practice for the following week was determined. This usually related to a certain thought or lesson from the weekly Torah reading. One of the fellows of the *chavura* was elected to serve as its secretary. Resolutions and enactments were adopted, and he followed up on them. In addition, once or twice a week, the secretary called a *reidel*, a discussion session. During this meeting, the fellows of the group determined whether their resolutions were successfully implemented and exchanged views and thoughts in an informal setting. The secretary would then comment with extemporaneous quotations from classical Musar texts, the Talmud, the Midrash, or stories of the Musar greats, and relate them to the topic under discussion. The session closed with a Musar talk delivered by the secretary or the leader of the *chavura*.

These sessions were not officially part of the yeshiva curriculum, although clearly they were a part of the experience. The main weekly meeting of each group, however, took place in the yeshiva building and consisted of a Musar discourse delivered by the group's leader. This lasted forty-five minutes. Each *chavura* met a different time; a general meeting of all the groups was held on the eve of the New Moon. A talk was delivered by one of the advanced students, followed by the afternoon prayer. This prayer was described as rivaling the Yom Kippur service in the intensity of feeling that it aroused.

Occasionally, a general gathering was also held whenever the spirits in the yeshiva appeared to be lagging. This was called *Va'ad Haruach*, and often took place in *Elul*. The purpose of this event was to awaken enthusiasm for Divine Service and to induce the students into accepting resolutions for personal improvement and development.

The Musar *chavura* was dedicated to three specific goals. First, to acquire broad knowledge of Musar works from previous generations. These included the works of Rabbeinu Yona, Rambam, Chovos Halevovos, and the classical commentaries on the entire Bible, such as Ibn Ezra, Ramban, and Midrash. Second, to explore Musar topics and to work on good character traits. Third, to gain familiarity and facility with methods of Musar study through emotional arousal and enthusiastic, heartfelt prayer.

Each of the fellows of the *chavura* kept a detailed diary. Twice a week, several members of a group would meet and discuss an episode that had happened to one of them. They would dissect the psychological underpinnings of each action, dispute its ramifications, and determine how that event should have been optimally handled.

The poverty within the yeshiva was extreme. Most of the students were refugees from Russia and had no means of support. Even those who received assistance from relatives gave it away to others in accordance with the Novarodok ideals of self-sacrifice and trust in God. It was said that an average Polish Jew might not know where his bread would come from tomorrow but, in Novarodok, they did not know where their food came from yesterday. Not infrequently, the meager rations did not arrive in time for breakfast. Occasionally, they did not arrive at all. During one period of several weeks, all the meals consisted solely of small mandarin oranges that had materialized from some unknown source on one particularly hungry occasion. The boys slept in the *Beis Midrash* and wore whatever clothing they had brought with them from Russia. The yeshiva students borrowed Rav Jofen's overcoat when they went to meet their proposed matches. The lady of one household, where such students often came, maintained this coat and made sure that it was cleaned and that all buttons were repaired while the prospective groom conversed with his potential mate.

All of the ways of Novarodok were continued in Bialistok. They studied and practiced Musar, the best students went into seclusion for private Musar study, and everyone gave up personal interests for the benefit of others. The yeshivas of Novarodok were an entire multifaceted world within the universe of Torah study—connected by inner unity of purpose, led by men of great accomplishment, with their will bent to the leadership of a single great personality, Rav Avrohom Jofen.

As it had done previously in Russia, the movement emphasized founding new institutions of Torah study. Every six months, several of the advanced students were selected for the privilege of being sent to surrounding towns and villages to found new yeshivas. They would stay several months and then be relieved by a new group that continued their work. These activities were guided by a set of principles that prescribed the methods and the framework to be followed.

The tens of thousands of Novarodok adherents had a profound effect on Polish Jewry. The fervor and dedication that they lived and breathed found a responsive echo in the chasidic world of Poland, which respected and looked up to the movement and its leaders. It seemed that the tide might begin to turn in the struggle with the Enlightenment, whose slogans were beginning to grow stale and to lose their hold over the Jewish masses. Who knows what heights the movement may have reached, had it only been able to continue to grow and develop?

# 8
# Flight and Rebirth

The Holocaust rolled over Poland in a fury of destruction. Of the four hundred students from the central yeshiva in Bialistok, most escaped to Vilna with Rav Avrohom Jofen in the summer of 1939. There they sought counsel from Rav Chaim Ozer Grodzinski, the undisputed leader of his generation. Rav Chaim Ozer was on his deathbed; he passed away only a few days later. With effort he raised himself up and whispered into Rav Jofen's ear, "When I was a small child, I heard it quoted that Rav Chaim Volozhiner said: 'the Torah will one day wander to America.'"

Nearly two hundred students remained in Bialistok with Rav Yisroel Movshovitz. This city was first taken by the Germans but was then handed to the Soviet Union, in accordance with the secret Molotov-Ribentropp pact to divide Poland. Rav Chaim Ozer Gorodzenski urged all the yeshivas in Eastern Poland to flee to Lithuania. One hundred and sixty-six students escaped from Bialistok to Lithuania that winter, first to Vilna and then, by decree of the occupying Red Army, to the town of Birzhai. They were joined there by refugees from other yeshivas and by Rav Avrohom Jofen's group. The Pinsk contingent, one hundred and twenty-four people, found refuge in Vilkomir. There were also refugees in the town of Nemitsin. Over a hundred students found themselves in Vilna (among more than two thousand other yeshiva students and an equal number of refugee youths from various

Zionist and secular movements); they were exiled to Siberia in the spring of 1940 (despite having received visas to to Sweden). Their offense consisted of declining to accept Russian citizenship, for this would have effectively precluded any chance of leaving the Soviet paradise. The story of the valiant struggles of these exiles deserves a book of its own. With superhuman strength and unflinching resolve, they practiced the ways of Novarodok in the most harrowing of circumstances inside the labor camps and battalions and exile settlements of the Soviet Gulag. Musar *chavuras* and meetings were held during daily marches to work sites and in the barracks after long days of grueling labor. The annual convocations were somehow continued. Resolutions were adopted and, incredibly, were carried out. There may have been no food, no clothing, and no heat but there was dedication and purposefulness of spirit. Rav Yisroel Movshovits served as the spiritual leader of these scattered embers of Novarodok. His wife and children were murdered by the Nazis and he, himself, was chosen as a special target for persecution and abuse by the NKVD secret police. Despite all this, he remained steadfast and strong and he led by personal example. Many of the exiles perished from hunger, disease, and starvation but many also survived and were repatriated after the war to the United States and Israel, via Poland. A number of personalities who remained in Poland were caught up in the Nazi extermination machine. The most prominent of the survivors was Rabbi Gershon Liebman, who, after the war, built an extensive educational network in France, Ohr Yosef. Rav Jofen himself, while still in Lithuania, was able to obtain a visa to Kobe, Japan, and arrived in the New World, together with many of his students, on the last ship to leave Japan before Pearl Harbor. After the war, he founded Beth Joseph in Brooklyn, New York. Many of the graduates of Novarodok yeshivas became leaders of Jewry in the United States, France, England, and Israel. The teachings of Novarodok enrich and suffuse the contemporary Jewish worldview, throughout the yeshiva world and beyond it. Novarodok influence extends far beyond its recognized sphere and continues to mold and educate us. The spirit of Novarodok did not die.

On one fine spring day in 1960, at the height of the Cold War, Rav Jofen was contacted by the State Department. A message came through supersecret channels, directly from the Kremlin: "The Kiev Jewish cemetery will soon be demolished and built over." The State Department personnel passed on this mysterious communique, although its significance eluded them. Neither did they understand why it was directed to an elderly rabbi in Brooklyn. Rav Jofen, however, surmised that a former student of Novarodok must hold a position at the center of power of the Soviet state and, out of loyalty to Rav Yozel's memory, wished to warn that his great teacher's grave would soon be disturbed. Rav Jofen engaged Rabbi Harry Bronstein of the Al Tidom organization, who, at great personal risk, traveled to Kiev and, despite KGB interference, succeeded in bringing Rav Yosef Yozel's remains to be buried on Har Hamenuchos in Jerusalem.

# II

*Selections from Madreigas Ho'odom*

# 9
# *Introduction*

The Sages said: "He who possesses Torah but does not have Fear of Heaven is like someone who was appointed to dispense charity and was entrusted with the keys to the inner chamber but not with the keys to the front door. How can he enter?" (*Shabbos* 31a). In this statement, the Fear of Heaven is compared to the outer doors of a dwelling; the Torah is within. This seems to contradict another passage that describes Fear of Heaven as being on the inside. "Rabbi Yanai announced, 'Pity on the one who has no courtyard but builds a gate for the courtyard'" (*Yoma* 72b). Here, Torah scholarship is identified with a gate that leads into the courtyard of The Fear of Heaven.

The answer is that the Torah is the inner substance of being and all of life's questions are resolved in its light. Whether they be questions of spirit or issues of the material world, the Torah encompasses all of man's considerations, his feelings, his habits, his aspirations, his needs. The Torah intimately understands man and has something to say about his every concern. Its teachings contain advice for every possible situation and circumstance; all is in it.

Man does not appreciate the true grandeur of the Torah. It is like an airplane which appears small to an observer on the ground because it is so very far away. He cannot imagine that there is space within for hundreds of people, facilities, and food and drink for all their needs. He might wonder: "How can such a small dot contain and provide for so many people, how can there be rooms and kitchens in such a small place, how can a whole 'world' fit in there?"

All this is because man is far removed from the true appreciation of Torah. When he sees it up close and enters within its portals, all such difficulties disappear. One who is far from it will ask many questions and raise many objections; our response must be "come closer and see"; as it says, "Taste and see that God is good" (Psalm 34:9).

But... man has not the outside keys to approach it, to enter within. His poor character traits are like a wall that separates him from the Torah. This is the gate to which the Sages refer. Without the keys of good character, one cannot appreciate the true nature of the Torah. This in turn keeps him from passing through it into the inner sanctum, referred to as the "courtyard."

Although a person may realize that his own shortcomings keep him from the source of life, he is not moved to give them up. This is described by the prophet, "and the wicked are like a raging sea, they cannot rest, and their waters spit out feces and tar" (Isaiah 57:20). Although the waves see that those which preceded them were broken uselessly on the sea banks, they continue to roll on their futile, predetermined path. Each one says: "We know why the previous ones were broken and why they have not succeeded. We can compromise and we will triumph; we will have it all. We will be stronger than they, we will flourish and prosper and we will achieve our goals." Still, they too end up broken on the seashore. Moreover, once they have tasted the corruption of the world, their good intentions are ruined and all the dirt and tar come out. From whence comes such blindness? From poor character traits and uncontested bad habits of men.

One who does not master himself and does not rule over his desires is like a peddler who carries holy books on his back. They do not penetrate his essence, for evil character traits prevent this. Such a person does not have the outside keys to let in the power of Torah. How can one benefit from its teachings when the desires for honor, envy and lust rule over him. One so compromised at the core of his being will only use his learning to realize lowly desires and objectives, as a "door" to get to what his selfish self wants. This is why no amount of Torah learning by itself can purify a person. This is why Musar is essential.

When people place the fulcrum of their lives, their interests, and their spheres of activity outside of the "holy," they cannot lead a proper Torah life; to them, the Torah becomes "a dot in the sky." The Torah becomes a means to accomplish goals that are in truth antithetical to Torah values, a means to material and physical enterprises. Eventually these fail and then it is the Torah, not ones's own foolishness, that is blamed for the lack of spiritual success.

A life of Torah must be lived in a community. A person who is alone can easily become discouraged but in a group he finds a source of strength. This is because impediments to perfection exist solely in one's imagination. The group assists the individual to "ride out" temporary problems and, of themselves, the mirages disappear and dissolve.

He who wants to run away from the Torah can find many distractions that will keep him from spiritual pursuits. "The time isn't right, the path is too strange, I cannot find colleagues to join me in this work," etc. He adds one difficulty on top of another until it appears impossible to go on. But, as surely as the eagle thrusts toward the sun, one who wishes to run after the Lord will find our times most conducive to the pursuit of perfection. Never before have we seen so vividly how the desire for compromise corrupts the most noble men and leads them to destruction. We have seen how those who have not accustomed themselves to withstand trials could not retain "the point of truth" and were lost in despair. We have seen how sweet dreams and noble fantasies led men to build exalted structures on foundations of vanity; all soon was gone—in storm, in sorrow and at what cost? On the other hand we have known those who have seen through the lies. They fought the "spirit of the times" and succeeded. We have learned these lessons well—one cannot blame the surroundings for one's own deficiencies. Again and again a fool repeats his mistakes. So it says: "If you grind a fool in a grinder, amongst sheaves in a thresher, his foolishness will not separate from him" (Proverbs 27:22). The problem is that the fool thinks that they thresh the sheaves, and not him.

For these reasons we brought these matters to publication and divided them into eleven sections.

The first section is entitled "The Level of Man in the Epochs of the World." This explains how our forefathers trod upon the path of spiritual completeness each in his own time until today. So we must also do and follow in their footsteps. The second section goes by the name "Correcting the Character Traits," for this is all that matters in man's life. The third one, "The Ways of Repentance," deals with the principle that, in an instant, a person can completely change his entire life (as explained by the Rambam in "Laws of Repentance," chap. 7,7). This is a spiritual verity, for there is no law in the Torah which does not base itself upon reality. The Day of Atonement is a proof of this concept for at a single point in time, at the day's conclusion, repentance takes effect and sins are forgiven.

The fourth section is entitled "The Paths of *Bitachon*," for *Bitachon* is the basis for the development of all good traits. Without it, man would fail every trial. The fifth, "The Purification of Traits"—to live with realism and not by the imaginative faculty of one's mind. We discuss one who speaks of ethics but who is inwardly estranged from them. Such a person is as if born blind, for he cannot see that which is obvious. He never purified his character traits and he sees the Torah only through the spectacles of his faulty character.

We called the sixth section "And You Shall Choose Life." This is to explicate Rambam's statement that the source of all illness resides in bad character traits and that the Torah is a cure for all spiritual maladies (*Shmona Prokim*, chap. 4). It also discusses the paradox of "the righteous who suffer and the evildoers who prosper" (*Berakhos* 7a).

The seventh is "Fear and Love"—to elucidate what is "tangible love and tangible fear"—of which it states "the fear of God is pure, it persists forever" (Psalms 19:10). This is contrasted to a Fear of Heaven which a person only imagines that he possesses and a Fear of Heaven which is wholly intellectual in nature. These serve only to fool the seeker and lead him astray. The eighth is "Seeking Perfection"; the ninth, "The Ways of Life." In it we explain that which Rav Yisroel Salanter said: "The way of the Torah is to be a 'normal' person. We are compelled by the special trials of our age, however, to separate ourselves from the world." The tenth is called "The Point of Truth," which explains that the nature of the searcher must be to relate to all things with neutral disinterest, in order to be able to choose only the truth. The eleventh is "The True Judgment," which teaches how those who are spiritually complete measure their deeds and how not to err through errors in judgment.

Recently, our teacher Rav Yosef Yozel brought to light a letter on the subject, "Leading the Many to Righteousness." In it he describes how in our times everyone is obligated to apply all efforts to influence others and to save potential "children of Torah" from the teeth of gentile cultures. We must plant yeshivas wherever possible as our teacher has done even during the upheavals of the war.

# 10
# The Epochs

### THE FIRST MAN

The story of the Tree of Knowledge, as told in Genesis, is filled with many difficult concepts. How are we to understand that Adam, the crown of creation, God's handiwork, transgressed His explicit command, knowing that the penalty for this was death? If it was but an error in reasoning (as stated in *Moreh Nevukhim* 1,2), why was man punished so severely? How could Chava believe the serpent's assurances more than God's explicit warning? What did she mean by replying to the snake, "*Lest* we die"? Did God not explicitly tell them that they will *surely* die (Genesis 3:3)?

The key to answering these questions lies in the fact that there are two ways of relating to evil. The first is a recognition that does not awaken craving for that which is evil, whereas the second one does. An example of the former is the way we think about opium. We all know that it is an extremely pleasurable drug. Still, we do not desire to join the ranks of its users. Our mind recognizes the danger of drug use in such a tangible way that we reject even the possibility of succumbing to it. Opium does not appeal to us at all. The compulsion for honor or possessions, however, is quite different. We may know that these drive the man out of this world (*Avos* 2,16), but the potency of this knowledge is not sufficient to impress it upon our inner selves and to rid us of these desires. The information remains purely theoretical and does not compel.

Adam's intellect before his sin was pure logic, unaffected by bias, by predispositions. What he wanted did not subvert his reasoning nor dim his apprehension of good and bad. He understood evil, perceived it, and yet would only do good. In this respect he was like an angel, albeit an angel in garments of flesh (Job 10:11). He was dressed in his eternal body as we are dressed in our clothes. Consequently, it can be written, "And they both were naked, the man and his wife, and were not ashamed" (Genesis 2:25).

In one respect, though, he was not like an angel. An angel does not have free will and cannot choose to do evil. This is because his coming into existence is in itself an act of goodness (*Genesis Rabbah* 48:11. Compare *Pirkei D'Rabbi Eliezer* 50b). Adam, although his mind was pure and without bias, was given the ability to cease being like an angel. He could, at will, live a life of struggles and choices. He could choose either a life of an angel or a life of a man. If Adam were to choose to lead a life without spiritual perils, then he must take care not to eat of that tree. In that case, he would always continue to perceive clearly the distinctions between good and evil. But if he pined for a life of choices, if he wished that desires and lusts awaken inside him, if he wished to wage war and to vanquish them, then he had to eat of the tree of knowledge. Immediately, longings and inborn biases would awaken and struggle with the intellect and its forces. If Adam won, he would rise higher than before, for the gain is according to the effort. He would again live eternally. If he lost and his instincts ruled him, then he would have to die, for he had become a body of flesh and could not live forever. The warning not to eat of the tree was thus not a prohibition but advice. The Holy One made known to man that eating of the Tree of Knowledge could lead to his death. This is also why Chava emphasized "lest you will die," for it was entirely possible that even after eating of the tree she still would not die. Eating of the tree was not in itself sinful, providing that they triumphed afterwards. On the contrary, they could reach even greater heights. It was in this vein that the serpent answered her, "You will not die but you will be like God, who knows good and evil"; that is, "Do not fear that you will fail the test of freedom, for you will certainly withstand it and gain even greater spiritual stature." He assured her that she and her mate would remain wholly unaffected by evil and would prosper.

We find in the thirteen attributes that *Hashem* is called "God who postpones wrath but surely will not acquit" (Numbers 14:18). God's awareness of evildoers and his retribution does not negate His qualities of forgiveness and mercy. One does not affect the other; in fact, justice and mercy support one another. It is not so with human beings. When man becomes angry or irritated, he cannot completely suppress his anger until some time passes. It takes time until he can "cool down." Until then, some traces of anger remain and affect his feelings. The serpent assured Chava that, even after eating of the tree, the newly incorporated cravings would remain a kind of abstract knowledge, as before, and not influence her thought processes. If so, she thought, the risk is small.[1]

Alas, this was not to be. As soon as they ate of the tree, "their eyes opened and they knew that they were naked" (Genesis 3:7). Before the sin, man was not naked; he wore the garments of his body over his pure soul. After he committed this wrongdoing, he and his body became one and now he was naked. Evidently, Adam and Chava now recognized their grievous error. Now there awakened new lusts that could not be controlled. Man sought to cover his body in order to somewhat still these desires.

God then said to man: "Who told you that you are naked? Did you eat from the tree from which I commanded you not to eat? Did I not tell you not to enter into the situation of constant testing? Therefore,

---

1. There is support to this idea in the following Midrash (*Genesis Rabbah* 21:5). Rabbi Papus taught, "Man has become like one of us"—like one of the ministering angels. Rabbi Akiva said to him, "Papus, enough! How do you interpret 'Man has become like one of us?'" He answered, "God set two paths before him—the way of life and the way of death. But he chose for himself a different path."

since you bequeath failure to your children, now that desires and instincts dominate you, cursed be the ground . . . for you are dust, and to dust you shall return, and death is decreed upon you."[2]

## NOACH AND THE GENERATION OF THE FLOOD

After Adam, a new era began in man's spiritual life. Now, for all of his days he must rail at his nature and fight his inclinations; either his intellect or his lust must rule him. The men that came after Adam were not properly able to contend with their great enemy and generation after generation, man's spiritual state declined. Finally man fell so low that the Creator regretted having made him and said, "I shall wipe the man that I have created off the face of the earth" (Genesis 6:7).

Even then, however, there was one man not bowed by the gales of the times. He was not afraid and did not bend before the winds blowing in the world. He exemplified resistance to the mores of his generation; this was Noach.

"Noach was a righteous man in his generations; Noach walked with God" (Genesis 6:9). Rashi comments: "Noach needed help to assist him." Noach, though righteous, did not achieve a sufficiently high level to stand independently. His cognition of good was not strong enough and he still needed God's assistance. He was the kind of person about whom the Vilna Gaon said:

> "Without God's assistance, he would be unable to conquer it [the evil urge]" (Psalms 37:33). When a man reaches the point of having done everything that he could but still is unable to obtain a lasting victory over his Evil Inclination, God does not abandon him. For the inner love and awe are in the hands of Heaven. (*Even Sheleimah* 5,3)

---

2. *Yalkut Shimoni*, Genesis 40. The failings of the subsequent generations were inherent in Adam's sin.

Yet Noach was unique. Even in that corrupt generation, he offered all of his abilities and powers to the service of God. Only with regard to inner love and fear did he somewhat lack and therefore needed God's support.

The Sages commented, "He believed and did not believe, until the waters forced him to enter the ark" (*Genesis Rabbah* 32:9). He believed in his personal spiritual ability but he did not trust in that bit which was up to God. This was an error contrary to that of his contemporaries. They did not believe and believed. They did not believe in their own potential but did believe in God's kindness. The people of that generation did not strive to accomplish because they undervalued man's abilities; they did not fear punishment because they did not appreciate Divine providence. Noach knew the power of his free choice but feared that God's assistance might not be forthcoming. His contemporaries, on the other hand, were sure that they were too insignificant to matter and that God would deal graciously with them, no matter how great their sins. Therefore, the very same waters that pushed Noach into the Ark, forced his contemporaries out of it.

For such is the nature of the trials that we constantly undergo. A test uplifts and exults the climber but brings down and lessens the one who fails. The experiences of the war taught us this truth. He who sought God's word survived the tests and was elevated by them and the waters pushed him into the ark. The one who did not was destroyed and driven out of the ark, in which he had stood with but one foot.

Although Noach was righteous, his motivation remains somewhat unclear. What moved him to rise above others of his generation? Our Sages disagreed about that (*Sanhedrin* 105a). They inquired: "What does it mean "in his generations"? One explained it as a manner of praise and the other as denigration. One states that had Noach lived in the generation of Avraham or Moshe, Noach would have surely been righteous. The other Sage suggests that only in that lowly generation could he be considered worthy. In the times of Avraham, Noach would not have been considered someone special. They did not disagree that Noach was in fact a just man (to which the verses testify—*Eruvin* 18b). At issue is what compelled him to reach these heights. One Sage says that the search for truth itself forced him to rise higher. Surely in the generation of Avraham, without all the societal distractions to divine service, Noach would have been even greater. The other view is that the desire for truth alone is not sufficiently effective. It can bring a person to achieve more than most others but not more than all others. However, Noach realized that when humanity and its morals are corrupted, one cannot choose to be lukewarm in his commitments. If one does not strive for the highest realms, he will sink in the mud. Naught will remain of his good intentions. Had Noach lived in the time of Avraham, he might have remained content with lesser achievements.

As an illustration of this point, consider a man who travels with a first class ticket. During peacetime, when trains are easily available, first class marks a wealthy man. However, in the time of war, all lesser compartments are full of soldiers and army personnel. At such a time, one who needs to go anywhere is forced to travel first class. This is because of necessity, not choice. Similarly, Noach was propelled to his great stature because he had no choice. The alternative was to descend to the lowest depths.

## THE TIMES OF OUR FATHER AVRAHAM

From Noach to Avraham, ten generations passed under cover of spiritual darkness and the inhabitants of the earth lived and died with no awareness of moral law. Not a single person chose to lead a spiritual life. Then an altogether different man appeared.[3] At three years of age Avraham recognized his Creator (*Nedarim* 32a). His father and his neighbors could not restrain the power of his questing. So strong was his ability to probe for the truth that it broke through the authority of the accepted "truths" and facile assumptions of all his contem-

---

3. Other men served God because they clung to a family tradition; however, there was not even one who chose to serve God on his own (Cf. *Sukkah* 49b and Rashi: *T'chila L'geirim*).

poraries. He sought and found God and his Torah. The Sages tell us: "Avraham fulfilled the Torah before it was given" (*Yoma* 28a).

He also attained clear insight and mastery over his inner self. Avraham is associated with the attribute called *Omek Hadin*, which Rashi to *Pesachim* 54b understands to mean clarity in judging one's own deeds. In other words, he understood how all aspects of his motivation interacted and led to action. The *Akeida* testified to this great achievement.

Satan can waylay a person in one of two ways. He first tries to prevent the performance of a good deed. If that doesn't succeed, he attempts to ruin the purity of the motive. The difference between these two manners of attack is that when the commandment itself is the aim, he throws barriers of hardships and tribulations in man's way. To ruin the genuineness of motivation, on the contrary, he lightens the difficulties. Satan whispers comfortingly into the ear of one who is under stress that, through doing good, one can also obtain honor, wealth, or other benefits.

We find that Avraham was tested at *Akeida* in both of these fashions. First, Satan set up a great river. Our Father Avraham, however, did not stop. He said, "I will walk with my simplicity" (Psalms 26:11), as is explained in the Midrash (*Tanchuma Vayera* 22, *Sanhedrin* 89b). He entreated, "Save me, my God, for the waters have come onto my soul" (Psalms 69:2). After failing in this, Satan attempted to destroy the purity of Avraham's motivation and to steal the merits of his ordeal. He said to Avraham, "I heard from Heaven that a sheep is for the burnt offering but Yitshak is not for the burnt offering." That is to say, there is no hardship for you here. This is only a show in which you act your part. You do not need to struggle within, for God will surely avert your son's death." To this, Avraham answered, "Such is the punishment of a trickster, for even when he speaks the truth, he is not believed. It is not true, you did not hear this from Heaven." Thus speaks the Midrash.

Avraham's tactics were determined by the situation that he faced. He could not deny the fact of the river in front of him. Therefore, he replied that one must proceed in simple obedience; the Creator so commanded and so one must do. One cannot turn back for any reason. To accept Satan's argument meant that the test was no longer a test and didn't require strength of will. To meet this challenge, Avraham had to respond with deep conviction that Satan's sly words were all deceit and lies.

Now, as then, Satan tries to dissuade man from serving his Creator. To sway our Father Avraham, he was forced to set up a river. Unfortunately, we do not rate such great impediments. For us, every little difficulty becomes a problem. To our hindrances we surely can respond, "I will walk simply." Our trials are the width of a hair compared to Avraham's river. Similarly, Satan had to use the truth (Yitshak will not be sacrificed). We, on the other hand, can be easily seduced with false words, promises of honor, money, and the like. We must remember that such assurances in themselves negate the possibility of their fulfillment. The Sages taught us that "all who run after great gain, greatness escapes them" (*Eruvin* 13a). The Vilna Gaon explained that this applies equally to spiritual and material pursuits (Even Sheleimah 2,10). Any reliance on this worldly recompense for *mitzvos* is counterproductive. Since this is a fact, we don't need answers like "Such is the punishment of the trickster. . . ." We should say to ourselves, "Is not all of his tempting through vanity and deceit?!"

Although Avraham did triumph over Satan, he still was not certain that his conduct was perfect. He could not be sure that there was not some minute measure of self-interest tainting his dedication. For who can tell why he agreed to bind Yitshak up in preparation for the sacrifice? Was his motivation completely pure? How, after all, could he avoid doing it? If he refused, could his son escape from some other fatal event that God might bring about? The Almighty has many messengers to carry out his will. The Sages also tell us that Avraham's eyes poured out tears (*Genesis Rabbah* 56:11); that is, to some degree he retained the natural feelings of a father. He sensed some resistance deep within himself. This led him to doubt the certainty of his inner commitment to God, until the angel cried out: "Do not send your hand unto the child and do not do anything to him, for now I know that you are a God-fearing man." The Sages explained that after being stopped by the angel, Avraham tried to at least draw a drop of blood.[4] Since he sought pure dedication all his life, at that moment he saw an opportunity to purify his commitment. To persevere in this most difficult moment was to overcome whatever personal impediments may have remained. After the angel spoke to him, there were in existence two contradictory imperatives. On one hand, God commanded Avraham to sacrifice his son. On the other hand, the angel commanded him to desist. By choosing the command that went against the grain, Avraham could have purified himself to the core and would have demonstrated that there was nothing that could keep him from serving God. Had he chosen the order to which he was naturally predisposed, the possibility of not having been completely purely motivated would always remain. To prove that his intention was free of any bias and influence, Avraham chose the first order after hearing the second one. At that moment, he realized that his nature could no longer hinder him. With that one decision he accomplished a complete and lasting victory over the inner self.

This is why only then did God tell him: "Now I have known that you fear God—this itself made you God fearing. Until now you were my servant in potential but not in actuality (similar to the potential of a child to develop to adulthood). With this decision you have purified your deeds and truly became God fearing."

This incident also demonstrated that, unlike Noach, Avraham did not require God's help to be righteous. In fact, the Torah testified: "My Fathers walked with God" (Genesis 48,15). He did not need assistance from Above. Had the power of evil held sway over him to any extent, what greater support could God offer than allowing him not to slay Yitshak. By choosing to carry out the original instructions, Avraham revealed that he did not consider the angel's intervention a form of Divine assistance.

---

4. The conflicting commandments allowed him to choose to obey either one and overrode the prohibition of manslaughter (Cf. *Yalkut* 22,101). At the same time, he attempted to fulfill both commandments by causing a drop of blood to be spilled. God, however, showed him that the contradiction can be resolved in another fashion (Cf. *Ishim V'Shitos* by Rav S. Y. Zevin, p. 66, in the name of Rav Chaim Brisker).

## THE REVELATION AT SINAI

Although our Father Avraham achieved the level of complete freedom from the powers of evil, he did not return to the level of man before sin. His reason was so strong that he could overcome all contrary forces. Yet there remained traces of human nature in the hidden recesses of his psyche, as we explained. The spiritual life of men of distinction, such as Shem, Eiver, and the patriarchs, continued in like fashion for many generations. Although they rose to great heights, the damage that the serpent did to Chava did not disappear from her descendants until the Revelation at Sinai (*Yevamos* 103a).

At Mount Sinai the nation was transformed into a state similar to that of Adam before he sinned. The Jews reached this level when they declared "we shall do" before "we shall hear" (Exodus 24:7). At that moment, they resolved to abide absolutely and uncompromisingly by the commands of the Creator, to choose only what the Torah asks and not to ponder whether to follow them or not. They were ready to carry out God's will as the angels do, without questions or doubts (*Leviticus Rabbah* 1:1). They resolved that "we will hear" was only to find out the details of what must be done.

In response, the Divine Voice proclaimed, "Who divulged this secret to my sons?" (*Shabbos* 86a). Who revealed to them that the great barrier to achieving completeness is that man seeks "hearing" before "doing"? Man wants to know how necessary it is, how he will be affected by it, and what he will gain by it. Who revealed to My children that, to achieve the stature of Adam before the sin, one has to plant in himself the foundation of "doing" before "hearing"? Then he will always be ready to do the will of his Maker. He will not falter and he will not question whether or not to accept his duty. He will surrender himself to choose what the Torah has chosen and seek only to know how to fulfill it. By incorporating this basic principle, the generation of *Matan Torah* reached the highest level available to humanity. As soon as they so resolved, the poison that the serpent had originally injected into all of Chava's descendants left the nation and all those who followed in their ways (*Shabbos* 86a Rashi, Mazlaihu).

The Torah testifies: "And all the people saw the sounds" (Exodus 20:15). The Sages explained that they heard what is ordinarily visible and saw what is usually audible (Rashi to Exodus 20:15). Their intellect became united with their other sense perceptions. There is seeing and more than seeing, hearing and more than just hearing. Physical nature is a partition that screens off the full reach of the intellect. When natural bias is nullified, previously unimaginable realities can be perceived. To give an example, even the lowest human being imagines that he understands a righteous man. However, the true conception of a *tzadik*'s inner world and nature remains far from the experience of a common person, who can only relate to it as if to a flat, unidimensional representation of an unfamiliar landscape, some kind of a photograph or a painting. This analogy is not especially apt, for the photograph is at least an accurate representation of what it portrays. The mind of a man who never lived the life of wholeness, on the other hand, is totally incapable of grasping a righteous man's inner life. This is what the prophet describes: "They hear but do not hear, they see but do not see" (Isaiah 6:9). Such a man cannot see or hear clearly. Had he tasted Torah life, then its tests would make him wise. But he does not agree to hand himself over to the Torah just like that; he wants to know first what it demands of him and whether he likes it or not. If such a person happens to be a Torah scholar, he thrusts his will into its teachings and, therefore, perceives only what suits him. The Torah, in turn, leaves his consciousness and abandons his psyche, for he has not tried to live by it with feeling and enthusiasm.

Such was not the case when the Torah was given. The Jews committed themselves without reservation and, in return, their vision was freed from the limitations that bias and bad character traits impose upon the mind. They saw in the same way that one hears. The analogy is to a wall or a barrier that does not prevent hearing from beyond it. The Jews were still physical beings but their senses were freed from perceptual limitations. They also heard the visible. A person may look directly at a gem or sapphire but not notice it because he has never learned to appreciate precious stones and knows nothing of their value. The people who stood at Sinai, however, decisively committed themselves to the Torah and therefore longed for its treasures. They heard that which is visible; there were no barriers to their understanding. They knew what they had; therefore, they valued it above all things. The Ramban wrote that falsehood cannot stand on its own, that evil cannot take hold in the world except through a kind of sleight of hand, an ability to deceive and create illusions. A street shell game depends for its success on rapidity of execution; the hands move so quickly that observers do not have a chance to see what actually happens. In this fashion, con artists fool the unwary and completely deceive them.

The Evil Urge does the same. Satan's power resides in rushing man to carry out an action right away, before he stops to consider and wonder about what he is doing. The deed is done and there he stands, deliberating after the fact. This is why the wicked do not repent, though they know that their way leads only to destruction and to a bitter end (*Eruvin* 19a). Their urge hustles them along while their better judgment takes its time. Their realizations are always too late.

In spite of the great achievements of those who received the Torah, they remained susceptible to such trickery. Satan confused and hurried them by making it appear that Moshe had died. He showed them a bier in the sky on the way to burial (*Shabbos* 89b). Had they looked carefully, they would not have seen what they thought they saw. The *eirev rav* was fooled (and made the Golden Calf) but the Levites remained faithful (Exodus 32:26). They waited, thinking that perhaps Moshe will return.

\* \* \*

"And they stood at the foot of the mountain" (Exodus 19:17). God held the mountain over them like a barrel and said to them, "If you accept the Torah—fine; but if not, there you will be buried." Rabbi Acha Bar Yakov said: "From here, there is a great rebuttal to [acceptance of] the Torah" [i.e., it can be claimed that the Torah was accepted under duress]. Said Rovo: "Even so, they again accepted the Torah in the days of Ahashverosh." (*Shabbos* 88a)[5]

---

5. Because of the similarity of the subject, this passage, which is from *Tikun Hamidos*, has been included here. For a precedent of such arrangement, see *Madreigas Ho'odom*, p. 104.

This passage is difficult. At Sinai, the Jewish nation became again like Adam before he sinned, and it divested itself of all material concerns. Why was it necessary to hold the mountain above the people? Surely they would have freely and joyously accepted the Torah anyway. More surprisingly, the Jews of Ahashverosh sinned grievously at the feast that he made. They were a much more lowly generation, with many spiritual shortcomings. How could people like that completely forsake their past, change and reorder their lives? How did it come about that they freely and willingly accepted the Torah, while those who stood at Sinai had to be compelled to receive it?

Let us consider the distinction between the just and the wicked. We are told that the Evil Inclination appears to the former as large as a great mountain and to the latter as a tiny thread of hair (*Sukkah* 52a). The intention here is that the Evil Inclination does not aim to uproot and negate all that is good in a person, all at once. This would never work. Instead it approaches shrewdly and with evasive tactics. First, it induces man to accede to a small thing, a hair's breadth of a compromise, something that to his mind will do him no harm and will leave no trace behind. If successful, it moves on to bigger temptations and slowly carries the man along. Eventually, it separates him from the Torah and destroys his life (*Even Sheleimah* 4,4).

The righteous, however, know what is coming. They perceive that the "hair" is in truth a great mountain for "today the Evil Urge tells one to do this and tommorow to do that until it tells him to go worship idols" (*Shabbos* 105b). They fear a "small" transgression as much they fear a great mountain. The wicked, on the other hand, are blind to these facts. They judge the danger only by its appearance and, therefore, pay it no heed. "Such a little thing cannot harm us," they think. They blindly slide down the path of evil until they are smashed by the mountain and die in sin's grasp.

Something similar has occurred in our generation. There are individuals who at first were drawn to the Torah and sincerely desired to keep and fulfill it but now no longer put on *tefillin* or keep the commandments. The Evil Impulse won them over in stages. At first they allowed themselves to read books that, to their mind, were not heretical. They delved into these only in order to strengthen their faith. From there they proceeded to works that were unquestionably heretical and injurious far in excess of any possible benefit therein to be derived. Gradually they descended to works of apostasy until they left religion entirely. All this happened because they had not noticed the hair's breadth that was about to become a mountain.

Yerevoam ben Navat, who sinned and led others astray, also went awry in this fashion. The Sages tell us that he did not want to stand in the Temple courtyard while Rechovoam, as a descendant of David, sat. This led him to develop an entirely new religious system and to set up images of calves to replace the Holy Temple (*Sanhedrin* 101b).

Shaul had a smidgen of diffidence that, albeit exceedingly minor, led him to transgress an explicit command of the Almighty (1 Samuel 15). So small was this flaw that the prophet Shmuel had to rebuke Shaul repeatedly before the king even recognized it. He spared the cattle of the Amalekites and blamed the people for forcing him to do so, because they wished to bring the spoils of war as sacrifices to God. Shmuel said to Shaul, "Did not God command you—go and destroy the guilty, the Amalekites?" Shaul answered: "I obeyed the word of God . . . to sacrifice to the Lord." Shmuel told him again, "Does God desire sacrifice . . . but to listen to the voice of the Lord. He rejected you from kingship over Israel. . . ." Only then did Shaul admit, "I feared the people and listened to their voice" (1 Samuel 15:16–23).

Even at the moment of his greatest failing, Shaul was fully righteous (*Ecclesiastes Rabbah* 7:33). Shaul was not a man who would consciously deny the truth (*Yoma* 22b). Until he was shaken by the awesome significance of the prophet's words, he simply was not able to grasp his own true motivations. He did not acknowledge the minute bias in his reasoning. As king, his strong attachment to his people made him unable to understand how his fear of them colored and affected his thinking. Only when Shmuel's words tore Shaul and the people asunder and set them up as separate entities did he realize what led him to spare the cattle of the Amalekites.

To conclude—keeping the Torah depends upon watching its hair's breadths. One who does not do so will, at the end, be crushed.

Why do the wicked not perceive this? The answer is that they do not percieve the mountain because they believe that they can survive under it. They labor under the illusion that it contains a hollow space in which they can live and prosper, for it is a "mountain in the shape of a barrel." They do not know that one can walk around inside it but . . . not escape from it. Those caught within are destined to die therein and "there you will be buried."

The seeker of truth sees this hollow structure and those that live in it. He knows that they are imprisoned there by the choices that they had made. This is like a fly and a transparent trap. The fly sees many happy flies buzzing inside a desirable container and is seized by the desire to join them. However, its end is to die there. So it is with the wicked.

The world may be compared to a city under siege. A righteous person has no desire to enter this city, for he knows that he cannot leave it. He watches his every step so as not to be caught inside of it. The wicked man, on the contrary, is impressed by the apparent freedom of those inside the walls. He does not regard the armies outside and the pestilence and evil forces within; he chases external appearances and is lost forever.

With this, we can now consider the difference between the time of *Matan Torah* and the time of Ahashverosh. At Mount Sinai the people realized that to reject God's words would bring the mountain crushing onto their heads. They knew this because of their penetrating spiritual insight, not through any personal experience of failing and sinning. They saw those under that mountain for what they were—little men sunk in the limitations and pettiness of their very material and very restricted sphere of existence. This understanding arose from their greatness; in other words, they despised the material world so much that any risk of being caught up in it was totally unacceptable. When their children entered the land of Israel and lost this sensitivity, their attitude changed completely. The hair's breadth of compromise no longer appeared to be quite so dangerous. In these new circumstances, one could legitimately renege on the acceptance of the Torah.

In the days of Ahashverosh, the Jews again learned the basic truth, by living through it. They thought that they would benefit by enjoying the king's banquet and that a little compromise would not do them harm. They were nearly wiped out in consequence. The people learned that only in Torah can there be victory and that any compromise leads to destruction. They accepted through experience the truth they had seen at Sinai. A lesson like this can never be forgotten for it is part and parcel of all spiritual failing and an experience shared by all true seekers.

\* \* \*

When Moshe descended from Heaven with the Torah, he had to teach it to the people. He sat and judged them alone until Yisro questioned him about it (Exodus 18). Moshe told him, "For the people come unto me to seek God." Yisro answered him, "It is not good what you do. Surely you will be worn out and also this people with you." Now, had they come only to arbitrate torts and damages, you would have been able to perform the task alone. However, you instruct them in the path that they must follow and in the manner that they must act. You teach each one according to his own inclinations and abilities (*Exodus Rabbah* 2:2). You must become familiar with each individual's makeup and the nature of each one's spirituality. This takes much time and great effort. This you cannot do by yourself. Rather, select outstanding men from amongst the people and educate them. Let them transmit your teachings to the common folk now and in the future.

And so Moshe did. He chose the exceptional men from amongst the people and educated them; they taught others, and their students in turn taught others. Each one instructed his fellow, and in turn was taught by him. Each one influenced another and was influenced by him. So it went until the time of the prophets.

## THE PROPHETS

The function of the prophet was to guide the Jewish people as a whole and to show each individual his own unique path. The Vilna Gaon writes that the prophet would tell each person what he lacked spiritually and how to correct it (*Even Sheleimah* 5,1). The generations of prophets were, however, very different from those of Moshe. In his time, all were familiar with the spirit of the Torah; all desired to learn from Moshe and from the officials whom he appointed. Not so in the time of the prophets. In those later times the people no longer possessed this elevated awareness and some even taunted and insulted God's messengers.[6]

Still, even if some disdained to learn, there were others to whom prophets imparted a shining vision of the way of God. The prophet could still lead men to repentance and warn them away from heresy. According to the spirit of the time, it was still relatively easy to accept the truth and to change according to what it required. (It is in the light of losing this ability that we must understand the statement of the Sages that, in our times, he who parts from idolatry will die quickly [Avodah Zarah 17a]. The explanation is that in our times a truly penitent apostate must forcefully wrench himself from all his deviant habits and desires. He has to go against the grain of all that contemporary society accepts about what man is and what he represents. The stress of such a radical change can lead to his death). The prophet drew down the spirit of holiness to the people, who were then enabled to easily progress to great heights from whatever depths to which they may have descended. The prophet could touch the unique essence of each individual and the source of his spiritual failings and turn him back to God. The incident with Eliahu and the servants of Baal illustrates this (1 Kings 18:39). Eliahu brought such a strong light to the people that they turned to God and easily left behind the baggage of their previous beliefs and misconceptions. After the last prophets, Haggai, Zechariah and Malachi, died, the Holy Spirit ceased (Yoma 9a). Then began the era of yeshivas.

## THE ERA OF THE YESHIVAS

After prophesy ceased and God's direct word became scarce, streams of new life began to flow. These were the yeshivas. The academies of

---

6. Jeremiah 26:9; 2 Judges 2:17–19; 2 Chronicles 36:16.

Sura and Pompeditha raised the spiritual quality of all the communities of the Diaspora. There was a connection between the yeshivas and the people. The nation realized that the source of truth was to be found exclusively in the yeshivas and that, outside of them, there was but vanity, error, and voidness. They viewed the yeshivas as a kind of reference clock, with a correct and true inner mechanism and a properly calibrated dial. All set their watches by it. Anyone who thirsted for God's word searched and sought for the truth there.

The yeshivas produced men who were complete in all aspects. They recognized God, were familiar with His laws and statutes, they possessed pure hearts, and they were heroes of the spirit. Their only desire was to set straight the measuring stick of truth in all their actions. No storm or pressure in the world could move them from their positions.

After these men left the yeshiva and entered the world, they sanctified God's name in every place to which they came. These people were a living proof that spiritual wholeness is a superior way of life. The world filled the yeshivas with many students and the yeshivas filled the world with spiritual accomplishments. So it continued, generation after generation. The yeshivas and the surrounding Jewish world were not separate and unrelated but, on the contrary, drew from each other and sustained one another. They shared the same spirit and beliefs. A person seeking the Torah did not need to seclude himself and struggle with himself in the yeshiva in order to spiritually develop and grow. He did not have to overcome the influences that drew him to the outside. On the contrary, the attitude of the world pushed him toward the yeshiva and its values.

Such good fortune, however, eventually came to an end. A time came when a bitter root bore evil fruit in the world. The accursed Enlightenment slew many of our best and darkened the nation's heart. It led to such a state of deterioration that the multitudes began to disdain God's word and those who carried and represented it. Thus a cleft appeared between the yeshivas and the world and an abyss opened between them. Once people began to sense that the contemporary worldly life and a life of the spirit could not be reconciled, they began to turn away from the yeshivas and from what they represented.

New leaders appeared and led Jews away from the path of truth. Under the influence of this new wind of "enlightenment," the spirit of dedication in the yeshivas became progressively cooler and cooler. The few who remained limped, as it were, on two crutches, simultaneously facing in two irreconcilable directions. They were dazzled by what the world appeared to offer but, at the same time, did not wish to let go of the great riches that they knew they possessed. Weakened by inner conflict, they were drained of resolve and began to compromise. The good and the bad became mixed in their minds. A new species of religious Jew came into being, one that lacked a clear recognition of the truth and was deficient in his ancestors' great capacity for self-sacrifice. Communal life became like a clock with a broken inner mechanism. Sometimes it ran too fast and sometimes too slow and it needed constant manual adjustment. Only by drawing on sentimental attachment to tradition and forces of insincere motivation could the machinery be kept working. Even that did not persist for long; in many places the whole inner mechanism disintegrated and only the dial remained. Communal life became like the clock faces that hang in synagogues to indicate the times for Sabbath candle lighting. When that time arrives, a person can mistake the dial for a real clock for at that moment it shows the right time. In reality, of course, it does not tell time at all.

It is obvious that such an atmosphere could not create men of true knowledge and pure hearts, who could inspire and lead others. As long as incomplete motivations managed to sustain a semblance of old ways, things ambled on after a fashion. To our great sorrow, even that did not continue for long. When the First World War broke out, all that was hollow and untrue was obliterated. A Torah-adherent of this new type was not used to trials and could not find the inner strength to struggle; all was impoverished and destroyed. Only rare individuals remained who did not throw off the yoke of Torah. The authority of the Torah was broken and the yeshivas were devastated.

What are we to do? The *Yetzer Hora*, the ideologies of "freedom" and heresy become stronger every day. They have begun to weaken even those few who remain loyal to the Torah and to attract even them to the values of the secular world. Seek then counsel to save the good, simple souls amongst our people. They especially are being swept away by the floods of the times that daily grow more powerful.

There is but one way. We must elevate the status of the yeshivas and return to them their original glory—not merely to their recent condition, for bitter experience has shown us that without an inner renewal the yeshivas cannot persist.

If we truly want to rebuild them, they must be set upon foundations of truth and lifted to the level of the academies of yore. To achieve this, a basic axiom must be laid down: "We will ask but one thing—to dwell in God's house all the days of our lives" (Psalms 27:4). This means that we will not be a part of the world, for it has moved too far away from us. Rather, we must begin to emphasize that the world and the yeshiva are at two contradictory extremes and that to escape the destructive influence of the world we, the few who remain, must reinforce our positions and move ever farther away from the world. At this time of destruction, when all trains are full of soldiers, we must travel first class. At this time of danger and desolation, we must squeeze ourselves even tighter into the four ells of Torah life; he who comes to join himself to God's inheritance will build there for himself a little world. There he will develop his talents and character without outside interference. We must, therefore, create an inner mechanism in each individual that forces separation from the outside world and we must choose the yeshiva as our sphere of activity. The yeshivas that will arise from this effort will be built only by those who are wholly committed to yeshiva life and yeshiva values. We cannot affect the world for, at present, it is in a state of confusion and rancor, buffeted by opposing and irreconcilable forces, in full gallop away from reality. There are but two options: leave the Torah for the world or create for ourselves a secure place of refuge in the midst of the upheavals that are taking place. This is not the time to be lukewarm in our commitments.

As the yeshivas rise, we can hope that the world will be rebuilt from within them. Under the exalted influence of the yeshivas, the honor of the Torah will be lifted throughout the world. From time immemorial the yeshivas have influenced the masses and taught them the way of truth. This is because the yeshivas proudly and enthusiastically carried the banner of Torah-true Judaism. When the spirit of the yeshivas sagged and their fire died down, the world deteriorated as well.

Adam was confronted with a choice similar to the one that we face in our generation. He could have remained a pure intellect and served his Creator with total commitment but he erred by seeking "great things." What did it lead to? "And they knew that they were naked" (Genesis 3:7). His example should teach us that it is a mistake to think that joining with the world will cause us no harm. Believing this is an error and in itself a form of compromise. Let us not forget the recent past. Those who attempted to combine that which cannot be combined had nothing remain of their Torah. Furthermore, they themselves eventually came to pour scorn and disparagement upon everything holy. The Sages said, "The one who studied Torah and left it is worse than all others" (*Pesachim* 49b).

To choose both the Torah and the world will lead to losing both. For us there is but the yeshiva and Torah. Even though our times do not seem conducive to spiritual pursuits, by our efforts the situation will change and evolve.

A person should not find it difficult to separate from the world, to restrict himself to a limited realm of activity and to commit his heart and senses to the pursuit of *shleimus*. Let him not worry whether he can keep it up. Such a radical step may seem irrational but, contrary to intuitive expectation, man is best able to withstand tests in matters that do not involve intellectual consideration and reflection. Man is more likely to lapse in keeping "rational" commandments of the Torah (the *Mishpatim*) than in keeping the laws which do not immediately make sense. Even among the latter, a person tends to stumble over the details that are more acceptable to the mind, such as the requirements that a citron must not be dry or that the phylacteries must be completely square. Even when King Solomon erred, it was in regard to the reasons for commandments (*Sanhedrin* 21b). The Sages understood this well. That is why they said, regarding nonreligious works of philosophy, "He who reads hidden books has no share in the World-to-Come" (*Sanhedrin* 100b).

We should also note that there are personal qualities that are universally valued. Everyone knows that to call someone a thief is an insult, while the statements that a person fears God or is trustworthy and benevolent are perceived as praise. This shows that people fully accept Torah values in the sphere of ethics; yet the Sages say that "most sin by thievery and all by evil speech" (*Bava Basra* 165a). Surprisingly, we stumble and fail most in things that are universally accepted to be immoral. This is because man's mind has limitations. His desires and leanings affect his perceptions and he measures with the "scales of falsehood" (Proverbs 11:1). Man's conclusions often differ radically from the truth of the Torah. He is unwilling to hand his judgment over to Torah's guidance, for he is afraid that he will then have to continuously sacrifice his body and his property and get nothing in return. He views the Torah as a cruel overseer that demands and takes from him but does not give back. The Torah has revealed to us, however, that, on the contrary, the "giver" receives and the "taker" loses. A person is afraid to give up his personal honor even to avoid profanation of God's name. The Torah's view is "He who runs from greatness, greatness searches him out" (*Eruvin* 13a). Man imagines that, by keeping commandments, he loses; the Torah says that no harm will befall him (Ecclesiastes 8:5). One thinks that giving charity is a loss of money; in truth, the giver gains both wealth and merit (*Taanis* 9a).

Similarly, man believes that by trusting God, he hands himself over to God's will. The truth is that it is man who benefits. Aside from being showered with material advantages, he achieves a spiritual greatness that is far more valuable than all the treasures of the world.

These misconceptions endure because one has not trained himself to live by what the Torah has chosen, without fear of consequences. Have you ever tried to follow God, simply and without probing into the future? You might be surprised by results. Most men are like a blacksmith who attributes his financial well-being to the fact that he had not chosen to be a goldsmith. After all, he reasons, he had been a blacksmith all these years and not once has anyone brought him a gold band to fix. The fallacy is obvious. Had he been a goldsmith, he would have been much better off financially than he is now.

And this is only natural. One who has never questioned his own way of thinking, has never placed his burden upon God, and has not negated his own opinion before the view of the Torah, perceives in life only contradictions and rebuttals of this great principle. Such a person stumbles most over the rational laws, for it is here that he uses his intellect to ease his "burden." He thinks that the Torah is some kind of a robber that aims to take from him and to make his life miserable. Needless to say, such a man cannot truly appreciate the Torah. The Torah provides joy and happiness in a very difficult world. The Sages rejected an *arava*, which is in the shape of a saw rather than smooth, for Torah's ways are pleasant and its paths are peace (*Sukkah* 32a). If you do not know the inner logic of the Torah, you cannot properly comprehend its laws.

A person may ask, "Is it really possible to reach such heights of dedication?" This question comes only from poor character development. The Torah doesn't ask for gratuitous sacrifices; on the contrary, it appeals to man to accept its goodness. One who doesn't hand himself over to the Torah eventually loses himself and his learning and stumbles in observing its laws. He who commits his whole being completely and wholeheartedly benefits immensely.

Should the seeker then ask: "Since giving is really receiving, one who achieves this awareness no longer gives anything; why then should he be rewarded? Also, how can one on this high level keep the commandments purely for the sake of Heaven and with no intention of recompense; after all, he knows that he will gain so much precisely by performing them. Doesn't this invalidate his motivation and detract from the purity of his devotion?"

The solution to this problem lies in the words of the Vilna Gaon: "Inner Love of God and Fear of God are the gift of heaven" (*Even Sheleimah* 5:3). Let a person commit himself to God and do his will to the best of his ability—the rest will follow. Divine help comes only after man makes an initial effort. One who sincerely wants to repent and to turn to God will be helped to make progress, whatever awareness may be there to retard him. It is similar to when a person repents despite knowing that he was not in the past able to hold fast to his resolutions. Such a person is assisted to overcome all the impediments anyway. Fear not, no one becomes corrupted by rising to a higher level.

The Torah commanded: "You shall build me a temple and I will dwell in your midst" (Exodus 25:8). This has been interpreted to refer to a sanctuary within a person's heart. If you build within yourself a heart dedicated to God's will, he will surely help you.

Thus the Torah wrote, "And you shall *take* for me a tithe" (Exodus 25:1). It did not command, "You should *give* for me a tithe," for giving is taking and taking is giving.

If we really wish to reach a high spiritual state, if matters of Torah and Divine Service are truly precious to us, we shall have no fear. We must give from the heart and give completely. Then our giving will be giving and receiving will be receiving, and God will be with us. Through us this promise will be fulfilled: "And you will make me a sanctuary and I will dwell in your midst" (Exodus 25:8).

# 11
## From: Correcting Character Traits

Many are those who have gradually drifted away from the Torah, not out of rebelliousness or out of anger, but in a mistaken belief that judicious compromise would actually advance their spiritual state. It is a kind of sin for Heaven's sake. Straying outside of the accepted boundaries is improper but . . . it is for a good cause. If we ask them, why do Torah and secular matters need to be combined, or why must the Torah be made to fit contemporary cultural assumptions, they will reply that this is a necessary evil. "Our way will strengthen man's belief and will make a person complete," they argue. They err, however, in trying to provide ammunition for future spiritual conflicts instead of the ones here and now. The truth is that our focus must be on the present challenges. It has been clearly proven that "doing before hearing" brings immediate rewards and energizes one's spirit. Insecurity, however, leads man to desire to control the future and to spurn the obvious present benefits for nebulous future gains. He would rather give up the sure present than compromise potential future advancement. This happens when people sense that their current spiritual state is less than successful and that their path leads to a slow draining away of all the beauty of their spirituality. Yet they can still take solace in the future. They take comfort in asserting that the future will certainly make up for all the sacrifices and compensate for all the shortcomings. An adherent of this philosophy will surely feast at both tables, will definitely attain all kinds of perfection, and without question will be able to keep the Torah in both wealth and ease. He will influence others in a positive manner for, as a paragon of achievement, his opinions will carry weight. How can a person deceive himself so completely? More amazingly, this delusion takes hold despite the fact that everyone knows that doing the right thing, right now and irrespective of the circumstances, uplifts and sanctifies God's name. Only the present can lead man to learn how to be good and to acquire a multitude of worthy qualities. But what he fears above all in making an absolute commitment is that his strength will fail in the future and that he will come up against trials that will force him off this elevated plane. This fear is what holds him back. The followers of the Enlightenment convince themselves that to combine Torah and secular pursuits is, if not fully meritorious, at least a sin for the sake of Heaven. After all, the Torah praises "a sin for the sake of Heaven" (*Nazir* 23a). Once a person starts out on the way of compromise, he is lost. Even after many years pass, even after recognizing that he ruined his life, he comforts himself with the thought that at least he labored in the proper way, upon the path that the Torah both permitted and praised.

Rabbi Avrohom Halevy ben Hisdai, in his *Ben Hamelech Vhanazir*, quotes the following parable:

> There was once a dog that heard of two weddings that were to take place on the same day, one in his own town and the other in an outlying city. "Well," he reasoned, "I can always make it to the local wedding. Let me first run to the other one and enjoy myself." By the time he got there, however, the reception was over. Anxiously, he sped back. Alas, he was late there as well. In his great bitterness, the dog began to bark and insisted on being given some leftover scraps. This earned him a well-deserved beating, which left him crippled for the rest of his days.

One cannot dance at two weddings.

Thus Solomon said, "God made man straight but they sought many calculations" (Ecclesiastes 7:29). At the time of Ahashverosh, the Jews were almost destroyed through pursuing religious compromise. They learned firsthand that one must act first and only deliberate afterwards and they accepted the Torah again as they had done previously at Sinai.

We are advised to learn from a buck (Song of Songs 2:9, Proverbs 6:5). When pursued, a buck immediately plunges deep into the woods. To avoid being caught in the branches, it breaks off its antlers and flees unhindered. A man must do the same and must react immediately. He must break off bad character traits and worldly entanglements to escape the inner enemy. What's more, the forest in which a man finds himself is purely imaginary. The man who feels constrained by the opinion of others and bound up in the chains of his circumstances, the man who worries about his social world—he himself is the problem. His own horns make the forest. In reality, this world contains no true obstacle. A man imagines difficulties only because of his bad character traits and predispositions. The nature of the *Yetzer Hora* is to create imaginary barriers. He who makes a firm, powerful decision to persevere will be obstructed by neither forest nor pursuers. We learn this from the buck—that one must fear only his own "antlers." There is no choice but to get rid of them. He who tries to uproot the forest, instead, remains imprisoned in the dark woods, trapped by his antlers, ensnared, bewildered, confused.

The truth is that a person can completely change in one moment. This ability is not a superior attainment that can be found only among the great saints; it is something that everyone possesses. If a man will not change now—when will he change? Why not right now? Should one wait until all his worries and troubles abate? There has to come a time when one must decide and must make the break with the past. Let it be right now.

The man who says, "I will do a little today and a little tomorrow," is like a person who has a *treif* kitchen. If he tries to substitute one pot today and another tommorow, all the utensils will become nonkosher, new pots through contact with the old ones. To kosher a kitchen one must change everything at once and without fear.

# 12
# From: The Paths of Bitachon

Internalizing the attribute of *Bitachon* leads to two benefits. First, he who trusts in God is freed from all the troubles of the world. He is spared the emotional fragmentation caused by overly intense involvement in too many worldly concerns. He is also saved from wearing himself out, body and soul. He no longer needs to seek benefactors, to flatter, to gain favor, or to sell himself for a bowl of porridge. The man of *Bitachon* can turn away from all of life's problems for he knows that he will not want. What he must provide for the needs of the body, he does in peace and contentment for he knows that no one can take away what the Creator allotted to him. In times of danger he does not tremble. He walks securely and does not fear for tomorrow, for as long as he relies on the Almighty, he has everything.

Second, he has acquired the habit of *Bitachon*, a path and a course in life. The direction that one has in this world is even more important than the benefits to which it leads. The advantages gained through *Bitachon* are only indicators of its supreme value and by no means its only measure. The prophet said: "Blessed be the man who trusts in the Lord and the Lord shall be his source of trust" (Jeremiah 17:7). He who is on a proper path is blessed with inner peace and it is the Eternal who is his refuge. King David said: "God is your shadow"

(Psalms 121:5). As man moves, so does his shadow; if he stretches forth a hand, the shadow follows him.

A man who trusts in God is assisted in wondrous and unexpected ways, ways that no one could have foreseen or anticipated. This applies even in times of danger, as described in the *Yerushalmi*:

> A proselyte who had once been an astrologer wished to go on a journey. He thought to himself, "How can I travel now? Isn't this an astrologically inauspicious time?" He thought again, "But didn't I join this holy people in order to get away from such matters, as it states, '... but for you, not so the Lord made your lot'—that you should not listen to magicians and wizards. Let me go out in the name of our Creator." So he went out. On the way he came close to being mauled. He gave up his donkey to a wild animal and escaped. What caused him to be endangered at all? Because at first he had doubts. What saved him at the end? Because he trusted God. (*Shabbos* 6:9)

You see from this that he who trusts should not turn back even when there is a known danger.

True *Bitachon* has the power to overcome and change nature. We find this expressed in the Midrash; it states that there is no generation in which there aren't those who are like Yakov (*Genesis Rabbah* 74:1). Now Yakov was renowned for such a great level of trust in God that nature itself was beholden to his will. We find that Lavan changed Yakov's compensation a hundred times. Still Yakov remained faithfully in his employ, with great trust that God would protect him. All of Lavan's machinations turned out for nought. Whenever he changed the agreement, the sheep changed as well. Even the lambs that were already conceived changed colors and patterns in Yakov's favor (Ramban to Genesis 31:8). You might ask: "If Yakov reached such a high level of trust, why was it necessary for him to resort to setting up variegated sticks by the water troughs? Doesn't this represent an element of human effort that, as we will explain, is inappropriate for a person of Yakov's stature?" The answer is that Yakov intended nothing other than to fulfill his obligation to Lavan through these sticks. They were designed to encourage the sheep to procreate. It is known that sheep go into heat when exposed to brightly colored objects. Yakov set the sticks up only after Lavan removed the colored flocks away to three days distance. He needed a substitute and employed this particular mechanism to encourage his flocks. Such is the way of the righteous—to seek to benefit others whenever possible. We do not find that Yakov was punished for lack of *Bitachon* in this matter. He was punished, but for a completely different reason. He said to Lavan, "And my righteousness shall testify for me on a morrow" (Genesis 30:33). The Sages said: "You mention tomorrow. Tomorrow your daughter shall go out and be violated as it states, 'And Dina, daughter of Leah, went out'" (*Yalkut Shimoni* 30,130). You see that this was his only failing in matters of *Bitachon*. This reinforces our conclusion that he used the sticks not with intent to help himself but to better carry out his responsibilities to Lavan.

Yosef was also punished for falling below his appropriate level. For relying on the wine steward, two years were added to his term of imprisonment. One wonders why? What is wrong with making an effort to escape to freedom? Undoubtedly, Yosef hoped to be reunited with his father and to learn more Torah from him.

To understand this, we must first ask why there is a disparity in the descriptions of "stumbling." On the one hand, we are told that "the righteous will fall seven times and rise up again" (Proverbs 24:16). On the other hand, we learn that "when one who commits a sin and repeats it, it becomes to him as if something which is permitted" (*Yoma* 86a). The resolution to this discrepancy is to be found in yet another source. "If you see a *talmid chochom* commit a sin at night, do not think badly of him during the day, for certainly he has repented" (*Berakhos* 19a). The specific terms used here reveal a solution and a lesson. *Talmid chochom* is literally translated as "student of the wise."[1] He is someone who has not yet found his way in life and is still experimenting with different approaches to Divine Service. At times he may even unintentionally stumble because of this, as can happen to any sincere seeker of truth. His fall, however, is a learning experience. Every blun-

---

1. Compare introduction of the *Peri Megadim* to *Orach Chaim*.

der becomes a light to guide him further. Each failing is an opportunity to change and to grow. A serious student will not allow himself to fail twice in the same fashion. Not so one who sees himself as no longer a student but a sage. This person will continue upon his chosen path, no matter what. He is rigid and settled in his ways and will not deviate from them, no matter what happens. For such a person, each failing obscures the right path even more. He is so committed to the correctness of his position that he will disparage those with a higher, albeit different, way and praise those who do as he does. The more he repeats his errors the more they become permitted in his eyes.

Yosef's mistake was not in asking "for you shall remember me" but in restating his request in the form of "and you will mention me to Pharaoh" (Genesis 40:14). He repeated his mistake. He had the chance to realize that he should not have asked the vain courtier for help, and yet he asked again. Therein lay his fault and his failing.

The essence of *Bitachon* is that man must not worry about the future. God will provide. To seek help from an intermediary is to cause yourself harm. Those who seek the path of perfect *Bitachon* have learned this from experience.

There was an unlearned fellow who eked out a bare living by digging and selling lime. He heard the holy Alshich extol the virtues of *Bitachon*. He said to himself, "Am I crazy? Since this works without the need for intermediaries, why should I break my back in hard labor? I can stop working and receive all my needs with no trouble. Why should I labor night and day to earn what would come to me anyway?" So he made a decision and stuck with it. He stayed by his warm stove and recited psalms all day. When his wife and children pleaded with him to take his horse out and go back to work, he responded, "Are you mad? With my own ears I heard from the holy Alshich that a man who trusts in God receives his sustenance without effort. Why then should I go out in the cold and sleet? Till now, I didn't know this but now that I know, why should I work so hard? You, also, my dear ones, trust in God." Soon they became destitute and were forced to sell the horse and the cart. The new owner went to dig for lime and found a treasure that someone had hidden in the ground and he loaded it into the cart. Barely had he finished, when a boulder rolled down from the hill and killed him. The horse returned to its previous master's home, as was its habit. The children discovered the treasure and ran to tell their father, "Your *Bitachon* has saved you, for we have found a great treasure."

The Alshich's students were quite disturbed by this occurrence and they asked him, "How is it that this man is greater than we?" He answered them with a parable: "A post sunk into hard ground will stand forever. A post in soft, plowed earth sways from side to side and does not stay in place."

The lime digger accepted what he heard from the Alshich without doubts and without reservations. He took it as if there was no other way to live but this. The students, however, were like soft ground, for "he who is greater than his fellow, his Evil Urge is greater" (*Sukkah* 52a). They turned everything over and over in their minds—yes and no and maybe. Should one really rely on a miracle or maybe one can't? The outcome was a "soft" *Bitachon*, an uncertain commitment, and it didn't work.

What must one then do? He must sink his post so deeply that it reaches virgin ground. He must nullify all previously held ideas and build new definitions that reach beyond the old ones. It is like a person whose house was robbed. The thieves broke off the lock to gain entry. Surely, he will not just put up another lock of the same type. What is now needed is a stronger bolt and a more effective latch. Similarly, if the old fences did not work, you must build new and taller ones that can withstand assault. While a man doubts and vacillates, he loses the opportunity to gain perfection. He forfeits the very things for which he longs. Instead, he must accept the Torah as it is—that it is so and cannot be otherwise.

Rabbi Yisroel Salanter wrote in his *Even Yisroel* that there are two types of *Bitachon*. There is *Bitachon* of *Chovos Halevovos* and that of the Ramban. According to *Chovos Halevovos* (chap. 4), one has to trust God while utilizing intermediate expedients, for it is forbidden to rely upon miracles. No doubt, the Holy One Blessed Be He can bestow kindness directly, with or without an expenditure of human effort. Still, a person is required to do what he can to minimize the need for direct supernatural intervention. In this view, King Asa sinned by searching for answers from the physicians exclusively and from God not at all. In other words, he was not faulted for inquiring of the physicians but for relying only on them. Even in this formulation, one is not permitted to do more than is minimally required. To expend more than the minimal effort is to lack trust.

To the Ramban (Leviticus 26:11), however, *Bitachon* means thrusting one's burden exclusively onto the Lord. The Torah indeed did say of a physician "and he shall surely heal," but for a servant of God it is improper to seek a cure through natural means. Similarly, for livelihood one needs to do nothing but trust in God.

It would appear that the first view is fitting for God-fearing householders and the second for those who dwell in the Houses of Study. Even the *Chovos Halevovos* wrote of a different type of *Bitachon* for the select few, those who "choose the service of God and choose to fear him and trust him in the matters of their world and their learning, to turn away from lowly matters and long for the higher qualities. The man who does not reject peace and does not run to wealth, such a person will not be subverted by his *Yetzer Hora* and will not be seduced by the enchantments of the world. God will bring to such a man his due, without struggle and without labor. He will provide for his needs and sustenance, as it states: "God will not allow the soul of the righteous to hunger" (Proverbs 10:3). Similarly, the Rambam wrote, in the end of Laws of the Sabbatical Year:

> . . . and not only the tribe of Levi but any man born into the world, whose spirit fills him with goodwill and whose wisdom gives him understanding to separate from the world and to stand before the Lord, to serve him, to know the Lord and walk straight as God has made him, and to break off his neck the yoke of many considerations—behold, he has become sanctified to be the holy of holies and God will be his portion and inheritance forever. And he will receive all his needs in this world, as did the priests and the Levites. Thus David said, "God is the portion of my inheritance and my cup, You maintain my lot." (Psalms 16:5)

Rambam's source appears obvious. The verse states, "You shall not cut off the tribe, family of Kehas." The Midrash explains:

> It is stated (Psalms 33:18): "The eye of the Lord is upon all who fear Him." This is the tribe of Levi who sit and aspire for God's kindness. But do not all creatures hope for His kindness? However, the tribe of Levi do so to a greater degree, for they do not have a portion in the Land of Israel. Therefore, they sit and pray that the land produce its fruits and that they then receive their tithes, for they have nought in this world but the kindness of the Holy One Blessed Be He. (*Numbers Rabbah* 5,1).

Some commentators want to change the wording to read "the family of Levi" instead of "family of Kehas" because what the Midrash says applies to all the Levites. We can also explain, however, that what the Midrash has in mind is not specifically the Kehatites. Their specific privilege had ended with the cessation of their service in the Tabernacle. The Midrash wants to teach us that any person is like any Levite in this regard. The verse commands us all not to destroy this quality of complete faith and trust that Kehatites possessed, which enabled them to carry the holiest vessels of the Tabernacle. The Midrash speaks to all Jews.

The Levites were provided with tithes only because they feared God and depended on His kindness. They threw the yoke of earning a livelihood off their shoulders and stood before God to serve Him. As it was then, so it is now.

Now, let us elucidate the principles of this *Bitachon*, which is right for the select few. Certainly, what is completely in one's power is not subject to the terms of *Bitachon*, for, by definition, these matters are in one's power. It is also self-evident that to say: "Why should I put my hand into my pocket to take out my money, let God hand it to me" or to say: "Why put food into my mouth—let God place it there" is simple foolishness. On the other hand, what is completely out of one's control surely requires *Bitachon*. What about the in-between circumstances. Suppose one has lent money and the due date for repayment is approaching. Should one trust that God will arrange repayment or should one act on one's own behalf? The circumstances determine these matters. A specific judgment must be applied to each specific instance and situation.

To think that a certain individual is the only one who can provide you a particular benefit is in itself not a shortcoming. If, in fact, there is no one else (if there are just the two of you in the desert, for example), then this person is clearly the means which Providence has prepared. Yet to believe that, even under such circumstances, there is no other way for God to save you is to lack *Bitachon*. Is there anything too wondrous for the Lord? Neither is it wrong to acknowledge that an individual has helped you in the past and to expect the same from him in the future. The point is that one should not place trust in that individual exclusively. Whatever comes, comes from God.

The method that is most appropriate for training oneself in *Bitachon* should be individualized. If you can approach it with indomitable spirit, you can begin from the hardest situations and move on to the more common, easier ones. If you are not so strong, start with the easy matters and advance forward.

*Bitachon* must be approached with all the resources of a person's intellect. Although it does say, "Trust in *Hashem* with all your heart, but on your understanding do not rely" (Proverbs 3:5), the Vilna Gaon explained in his commentary to Proverbs: "Even as a mere support, do not rely upon your intellect." What this means is that a God fearing man should trust in God without using the prop of abstract reasoning. The reasoning should be based on Torah precedent. In general, all actions should be based solely on the Torah's logic and its commandments. The verse continues, "Refer to God in all your ways." We are admonished to be strong and courageous and never to amend His commands on the basis of pure intellectual reflection.

*Bitachon* also applies to those who occupy themselves with public service. However, if one engages in communal work without pay, the more effort he applies the better. In this area, you can't trust in God and sit back waiting for things to happen. If, on the other hand, one is being compensated by the community for his efforts, *Bitachon* is most necessary. In other occupations, there are the requirements of the marketplace and some degree of internal policing. In community service, usually no one looks over your shoulder and the decisions are all yours to make. Without deep faith, you may be led to very undesirable consequences. You may tolerate certain things for fear of controversy and you might lose sight of the fact that everything is in the hands of Heaven (*Kesubos* 30a).

You need to trust in God to finish what you have started. Shaul, the anointed of God, was as pure as a one-year-old child and had not tasted sin. Yet he was led to apply a faulty argument to spare the Amalekites (*Yoma* 22b). This was done in righteousness, for the verse testifies of him: "Do not be righteous overmuch" (Ecclesiastes 7:16). He was so sure of the correctness of his cause that he greeted the prophet Shmuel with the words "I have fulfilled the word of God" (1 Samuel 15:13). How much more wary must we be! We, who are susceptible to blandishments of personal interest, cannot succeed unless we trust Him to bring our efforts to a worthy conclusion.

One even needs *Bitachon* to acquire *Bitachon*. Even in this, one can fall into the trap of "my strength and the power of my hand" (Deuteronomy 8:17).

# 13
# From: *The Ways of Life*

Let us look at why Yitshak originally planned to bless Eisav rather than Yakov (Genesis 27). From the account given in the Torah, it appears that he tried to make certain that it was specifically Eisav, and not Yakov, who was standing in front of him. Yitshak said, "The voice is the voice of Yakov but the hands—hands of Eisav." Had Yitshak known this son to be Yakov, he would not have blessed him. What then did he mean by saying at the end: "Also blessed he be"? It seems that he changed his mind. What caused this? Furthermore, why was it necessary for Yakov to obtain the blessings through trickery? Couldn't he simply purchase them later from Eisav, as he did with the birthright?

If we think about Eisav's nature, we can learn some valuable lessons. The Torah tells us that after he swallowed the red (*edom*) food "therefore he called his name Edom." The Sages relate that Eisav committed five serious transgressions on that day (*Genesis Rabbah* 63:16), including murder and immorality. Why then did the Torah disparage him only for eating red beans, admittedly a much lesser fault? After all, by thirstily imbibing the red stew he hurt only himself, for he revealed his gluttony to all. In committing murder, he harmed others. Also, why, after Eisav cried, "Stuff me from this red, red," did Yakov immediately offer to buy the birthright? How did he know that this was an opportune moment for such a deal? Wouldn't Eisav want to remain the firstborn notwithstanding his craving for the tasty dish?

The Sages explain that, contrary to the superficial reading of this narrative, Eisav weighed the matter carefully. He asked Yakov, "What is the nature of this birthright?" (Rashi to Genesis 25:32). Eisav did not hand it over without reflection. How then was it that "and he ate and he drank and Eisav despised the birthright" (Genesis 25:34)?

It is known that recognizing distinctions shows the presence of the sense that is needed to do so. To choose white instead of black shows that one can see; to distinguish bitter and sweet defines the presence of the sense of taste. So it is said, "If there is no knowledge, from whence comes the ability to make distinctions?" (*Yerushalmi Berakhos* 5,2). He who cannot distinguish between good and evil and between true and false does not possess spiritual discernment. Such a man follows only his gross senses. For an elevated person, all perception depends upon his spiritual determinations—the greater the man, the finer his power of recognition.

Eisav came from the field and all he saw was a bowl of red beans. The Sages say that Avraham had died on that day (*Bava Basra* 15a). Beans are eaten by mourners, for they allude to the cycle of birth and death by their round shape and awaken sorrow and a sense of mourning. Yet Eisav said, "Give me from this red, red. . . ." He saw the most salient characteristic of the food—its color. He did not regard the shape. This first impression aroused hunger—not thought and not reflection. Because of this, Yakov called Eisav *Edom*—for it was the redness of the stew that caused all of the subsequent events and led to his complete spiritual ruin.

The truth is that such is the nature of sin in general. The desire arises from the first impression of the senses and seizes a person in its grasp; then there is no longer time or opportunity to reconsider. It proceeds to develop into an unstoppable passion and breaks through all barriers. The sinner then finds excuses for his shortcomings. Eisav said, "For here I go to death." The Sages said that he was told about prohibitions and punishments linked to the birthright by priestly services, such as, "These are culpable to death: those [who serve in the

Temple with] uncovered heads and drunk on wine" (Rashi to Genesis 25:32). Driven by his desire, he portrayed his unwillingness to comply with the obligations inherent in the birthright as a form of piety. Eisav excused himself with the hypocrisy that he did not wish to take on obligations that he might not be able to fulfill. This is like a person who, frightened by the sound of thunder, hides from it under covers and pillows. Such behavior, on a deeper level, comes from man's desire for honor and from his envy of others. A person cannot bear to be lower than others, so he invents a reason to turn his spiritual cowardice into a virtue. He makes it appear as if he is distressed by the loss of an opportunity to be elevated but . . . for the sake of Heaven, reluctantly, he must do so. The truth is that he simply does not wish to be elevated. It is not hard to be attracted to the truth, yet it is difficult to separate from falsehood.

When Yakov saw this, he knew that Eisav was in the throes of his inclination and would stop at nothing in his attempt to get the bean stew. This was an opportunity to buy the birthright (which Eisav now despised)—all for a bowl of red lentils. Throughout history it has remained so; Eisav sees the externals while Yakov perceives the heart of existence.

Thus, it is now even more surprising that Yitshak wanted to bless a person like Eisav. This becomes clear if we look deeper into the Torah. We discover two approaches to serving God. The first one is that of a social man, a man of community (*ish midini*), who, at the same time that he fulfills the Torah, is able to be involved with business and vocation. This kind of a person is personified by Yakov, who said of himself, "I sojourned with Lavan but kept the 613 commandments" (Rashi to Genesis 32:5). The sophistry of Lavan did not affect Yakov. He sojourned there. He did not loosen or compromise his observance of the 613 commandments and did not vitiate his dedication to the teachings of his forefathers. This type of man is very vigilant not to be involved in dishonesty or thievery. Yakov served Lavan with integrity despite the latter's machinations. One must fear no one and be unwavering in one's commitments if one wishes to be an *ish midini*. To succeed on this path, one must be willing, upon a moment's notice, to give up all that one has accomplished, for the sake of principle, and turn back to being the second type of man—the one of whom it is said: "Bread and salt you shall eat and on the earth you should sleep, while in Torah you toil" (*Avos* 6,4). This second approach is defined in the words of Rabbi Yisroel Salanter: "In the way of the Torah, the ideal is to be *ish midini*, but, perforce, one who wishes to lead a life of true spiritual perfection must be separate." What he means is that when a person is in a lowly state, his inclination is strong but his intellect is weak and undeveloped. Such a man cannot withstand temptation. A person like this should remove himself far from temptations. Of this, it says, "What a hero loses through his heroism, a weakling can obtain through his caution." The tried path to overcoming spiritual dangers is to avoid them. The Torah is like a pharmacy. Some medications are suited for certain illnesses and not for others. The effectiveness of a remedy depends upon proportions and ingredients, as well as on the patient's sickness and constitution. A person must take from this pharmacy only according to the advice of a wise teacher. What is good for one patient is dangerous for another (*Kuzari* 1,7). What Rav Yisroel said is that in our days the proper way is to seek out only the company of wise and learned men, men who themselves constantly seek the truth. To place yourself in other company before you are ready is fraught with certain danger. The nature of life's tests is that one who is low and fails can then fall very, very low.

This is why Yitshak wanted to give the blessings to Esau and not to Yakov. Yitshak thought that the older brother served God as *ish midini*. He reasoned that Eisav gained his livelihood from hunting, an occupation that did not involve other people's property, which obviated the problems of dishonest business gains. Nor was a hunter dependent on others. Eisav could therefore serve God as a man of the land, despite his weaknesses, with little danger to his spirituality. Yakov, on the other hand, separated himself from society in his House of Study. Yitshak thought that the brothers would complement each other in Divine Service. If so, then Yakov did not need the blessings.

From: The Ways of Life

His brother was the one in greater spiritual jeopardy and the blessings, therefore, were meant for him.

When Yitshak heard from Eisav "he also took my birthright," the error became obvious. He realized the true nature of his sons: that Eisav was a simple person whose heart followed his eyes and that Yakov was a sophisticated man who, with all his Fear of Heaven, also knew how to deal with the world. Then Yitshak said, "Also blessed he shall be."

# 14
# From: Leading the Many to Righteousness

When a good man realizes his imperfections, he is aroused to seek a way to correct himself. He does this according to how much he understands. He tries everything to bring this goal closer and is constantly preoccupied with it. In the same way, man must gather strength to step into the breach when he sees the great damage that resulted from the faulty education of the new generation. In our days the ideology of rebelliousness has spread even to the youngest children. All of the ways of the Torah lie desolate. There are but a few precious souls who remained at their posts and did not flee. Everyone knows that, if there are no kids, there will not be goats (*Genesis Rabbah* 42,4). If this is so, God forbid, in time Torah may come to be forgotten in Israel. Therefore, each of us must rise out of his slumber and see what is in front of him. We must go forth with all our strength and might, to do all that we can and all that is in our power.

This obligation devolves especially on those who study Torah day and night, those who understand the greatness of spiritual completeness and the emptiness of corrupted systems of contemporary education. Faulty teachings spread only because there is no opposition. Do not avoid these obligations with any excuse, reason, or circumstance, and regret not the time taken from your own spiritual work. The survival of the community is at stake.

Many excuses are offered because of muddled thinking. To elucidate the issue, let us pose ten questions about benefiting others.

1. Is there a specific regimen that will produce qualified workers to help the community?
2. Must one even engage in physical labor, if necessary, to accomplish these goals?
3. Can one delegate this work to the great men of each generation and consider oneself exempt?
4. Is there any other way in which one can exempt oneself?
5. Does the Torah require that one travel from place to place in order to spread Torah?
6. Is it in the power of individuals to affect the whole world solely by means of their spiritual conviction, and nothing else?
7. Is an educator required to examine all that concerns the youth and investigate their ways of behavior and thinking in order to correct them?
8. Is labor on behalf of others a contradiction to spiritual work for oneself?
9. Must one thoroughly understand people before acting for their benefit?
10. What about the person who wants to work for the public but refuses to accept the responsibility for the outcome?

Answers (extensively abridged and summarized):

1. Yes. Rabbi Chiya pursued such an educational regimen (*Bava Metziah* 85a)
2. Yes. Rabbi Chiya did so.
3. No. A student can often reach people and places that a greater man might not be able to reach and thereby can accomplish great things. Therefore, Rabbi Chiya involved his students in teaching each other.

4. Yes. Only someone who is especially gifted, like Rabbi Chanina, and can turn the hearts of people to Torah solely through his wisdom and intellect can invoke such an exemption. Such people are extremely rare. All others are absolutely obligated (*Bava Metziah* 85a).
5. Yes. Seventy thousand Jews were killed in Giveah because the great Sanhedrin did not travel from town to town to teach people Torah (*Tanna D'Bei Elliahu*,11).
6. Absolutely. Elkanah singlehandedly revived the *Mitzvah of Aliya Lregel* and it is considered as if he had saved the whole world (*Yalkut Samuel* 1).
7. Yes. The prayers of a *melamed* who did so were answered before those of the great *Amora* Rav, as related in the Talmud (*Taanis* 24a).
8. There is no contradiction. One who does for others himself earns merit and is blessed with great advances, as is described in regard to Rabbi Preida (*Eruvin* 54a).
9. From the story about Rabbi Preida and from common experience, we see that one need not seek deep psychological insight and sophisticated approaches before acting. One who engages others with a sincere desire to help, and does so in a straightforward and simple way, succeeds.
10. One must accept the responsibility and only then will he merit Divine assistance and prevail. One succeeds not because of his talents or abilities but only because he accepts the responsibilities of being a leader.

# III

*Rav Yosef Yozel's Life and Teachings*

# 15

# The Legacy of Rav Yosef Yozel

The Alter was known for his unique ability to deflate and criticize all the things that go on in the world. He could destroy and obliterate universally accepted notions of what was necessary, and good, and fitting. He nullified the value of all the imaginary things in which men take pleasure and, with convincing and palpable reasoning, showed them to be small and insignificant. He made honor and respect unappealing, as defined by a fickle and false society. The Alter tore off the beautiful, multicolored plumage and revealed the emptiness and nakedness that was at its core. He exposed it all as an empty vessel that held nothing desirable. Through his sharp insight he penetrated that inner essence of humankind that is enslaved by passion and hitched to the wagon of lust. He demonstrated that those who exhibit themselves as happy and triumphant in their intellectual mastery and who speak mighty words from their high tower of certitude are nothing but envious and bewildered people, desperate in pursuit of a mirage. His sharpness allowed him to fully fathom the narrow, crooked paths of confused men, who are petty and limited of vision. Like a wise businessman he stood afar and observed the small-minded shrewdness of the "freethinkers" who rushed about in the costumes of benevolence and charity but, in truth, were but "snakes on the road." In all of this he was truly unique in his generation.

Those who were *zocheh* to be close to Rav Yosef Yozel and to gain from him, clearly recognized his great power to tear down and to clear away. They related how he freed them from worry about worldly success, anxiety about making a living, and concern about settling down and participating in the affairs of this world. Instead, the Alter conveyed to them his vision of Divine splendor and that to yearn for matters of this transient abode is unworthy. Many are those who glimpsed his back, who were inspired through his power of negation and opposition. Few were those who came close enough to see the affirmation within the negation; fewer yet have truly grasped his greatness.

What the Alter asked of himself, what he sought with utmost effort to hide from others, what he has achieved above all, was his faith and trust in God and his uncompromising commitment to live 100 percent according to the teachings that Novarodok enunciated. His self-sacrifice gave him pride and strength of spirit and led to an iron determination to spread Torah throughout the length and breadth of Russia. He knew no rest and allowed no obstacle; he did not recognize limits, did not measure distances, and never said "enough" of Torah and its ways.

(Rabbi A. Jofen, as quoted in *Zachor L'Avraham*)

\* \* \*

When his father passed away, Rav Yosef Yozel thought that he detected in himself a smidgen of satisfaction from the thought that he would now inherit his father's extensive library. He immediately made a vow to receive no benefit from any of his father's possessions.

A visitor arrived at his house one morning to find the door off its hinges and Rav Yosef Yozel sleeping on it, covered by his coat. A student lay asleep on the *Rosh Yeshiva*'s bed.

His wife related that every Friday afternoon he returned from the bathhouse without a shirt. Each time he would offer an explanation of how it was lost; in truth, however, he always gave it away to one of the poor.

His students told many stories that illustrated how free he was from the preoccupations and concerns of other men.

To help the yeshiva, he would pawn his *Shabbos* coat, as well as his pillows and blankets, during the week.

Once, a student who lacked funds to travel home came to him. There was not a penny in the house and Rav Yosef Yozel handed him his daughter's engagement ring to sell and to use the proceeds to buy the ticket.

He took food for himself and his family only after all the students were fed. If there was not enough to go around, he skipped the meal.

After the first floor of the yeshiva in Novarodok was built, his family was asked to move into it until the second floor could be completed. When Rav Yosef Yozel discovered this, he ordered that the Musar hall be opened there instead and moved his family into the second floor, which was still under construction.

He was free from any sense of self-importance. He always served himself and always traveled third class, among the crowds of common folk. When not in the yeshiva, he prayed in the back of the synagogue, with the poor and the beggars. Because of this, he was once asked to hold the Torah scroll during the *Haftora* reading (this duty was usually given to children and people of little importance). From that time on, he always insisted on performing this "honor" himself. He never allowed a student to serve him or accompany him. He avoided public gatherings or receptions in his honor. On one occasion he switched trains to avoid a customary welcoming reception that was awaiting him in Rostov's central train station.

The Alter would not tolerate being called Rebbe and would not allow anyone to serve him. He would say that man was created with two hands to be able to take care of himself fully. Had his own abilities not been sufficient, man would have been given a third hand. He not only avoided honor, he sincerely did not care whether he was being honored or insulted. Rav Yosef never concerned himself with impressing others or with the personal consequences of his actions. "One must do what must be done" (13 *Middos of Rabbi Yisroel Salanter*). On one occasion, he rebuked a student who was worried about what others thought of him by quoting the *halacha* that requires a person who finds the biblically forbidden mixture of wool and linen in his garment to take it off, even in the street (*Berakhos* 19b). The student asked Rav Yosef Yozel whether he could find it in himself to disrobe in public. Rav Yosef Yozel answered, "Yes" and, to prove it, started to take off his coat right then and there in the street. His student barely managed to stop him.

He explained the statement in *Niddah* 30a, "Even if the whole world says to you that you are righteous, be wicked in your own eyes," as follows: "Even if everyone says you are righteous, let it be in your eyes as if they say you are wicked. Let praise and insult be the same to you."

A student visited his chasidic relatives and was very impressed with the reverence and honor that they showed their Rebbe. He therefore resolved that he would call his teacher "Rebbe" as a sign of respect. Rav Yosef Yozel objected, but to no avail. The boy took great pleasure in treating his teacher as a chasid treats his rabbi. Rav Yosef Yozel, however, disdained honor and, when nothing else worked, he threatened the student with expulsion if he persisted.

He was in Bobruisk on Yom Kippur, when wearing leather shoes is prohibited. There he saw a man in rabbinic garb who was wearing such shoes. The man explained that he had no socks and was ashamed to be seen without shoes. Rav Yosef Yozel then gave him his own socks and went through the rest of the day barefoot. To his relatives, he explained, "This man lives here and may be embarrassed by having to walk barefoot. No one here knows me, however, and so there is no room to be concerned about what the people think."

Someone told him about an incident where a man had bitterly insulted a friend in public. A bystander had commented that one who shames another Jew in public has no portion in the World-to-Come. The offender replied: "It is worth it to lose one's portion in the future world to show what a rascal he is." "Would he be willing to give up even a bit of *this* world for this purpose?" retorted Rav Yosef Yozel.

Rav Yosef Yozel participated in a Musar gathering with Rav Simcha Zissel Ziv and Rav Yitshak Blaser and their students. The rarefied atmosphere was filled with words of Torah and the participants felt transported to another plane of existence. Suddenly they heard lips smacking and the loud voice of Rav Yosef Yozel: "Ah, this butter is good. What a pleasure!" The onlookers turned to each other in amazement, obviously thinking, "Who is this uncouth man who is not moved by this splendor and cares only for his butter?!" Many years later Rav Yosef Yozel explained that he had lowered himself in this manner in order to break his desire for honor.

A great scholar came to visit him during a meal. When Rav Yosef Yozel perceived that he was being scrutinized, he lifted a plate of soup to his lips and loudly slurped it down. He did this to lower his standing in the visitor's eyes and to hide his own stature.

A visitor asked him, "Why have you chosen a way to spiritual advancement that appears to be so crooked?" Rav Yosef replied, "When one needs a ladder to climb upward, perforce it has to be set on a slant."

He avoided physical pleasures, not for the sake of asceticism but because he considered them utterly worthless.

Rav Yozel used to say, "One must always be in motion." He never rested. He was always busy, with enthusiasm and with feeling. He often said, "Where others mail a letter, I send a telegram; where others cable a telegram, I send a messenger; when a messenger is needed, I go in person." He never concerned himself with whether a particular project could be accomplished, only whether it was necessary.

Rav Yosef Yozel learned of a workshop where Rabbi Yisroel Salanter had worked, when he was ill and had been told by physicians to engage in manual labor. Wishing to learn more about how Rav Yisroel related to other workers, Rav Yosef Yozel walked seven kilometers to the workshop and discovered that Reb Yisroel told the other workmen that man must study Musar. After he returned he realized that he had forgotten the exact words that Rav Yisroel used, and he walked back again to clarify whether he had said "one must study Musar" or "one needs to study Musar."

Even in his old age he would not use a walking stick. He did not wear especially warm clothing or a scarf in the winter. He claimed that man is forbidden to allow himself to become old. Correspondingly, his age was not noticeable. On the contrary, his great physical prowess became especially prominent when he became older. He traveled constantly and tirelessly labored on the behalf of the yeshivas, notwithstanding his advanced age.

When the students of Novarodok "took over" the synagogue of the town of Konutov and converted it into a house of study, some of the householders complained to the Chofetz Chaim. The latter responded, "I testify about him (Rav Yosef Yozel) that all his actions are for the sake of Heaven." In another version, the Chofetz Chaim said this when certain individuals complained to him about Musar periods for young boys at local Novarodok schools. The Chofetz Chaim then added, "The study of Musar is something which is needed both by adults and by youngsters."

Rav Yosef Yozel's students said that even in the midst of giving the harshest rebuke he would pause to examine himself for any trace of anger. He knew how to push a confrontation only as far as necessary and would always pacify his opponent afterwards and part from him in friendship. After one such dispute, when reaching common ground appeared impossible, he left his coat behind to serve as an excuse to return again.

When Rav Yosef Yozel rebuked a student, he periodically stopped to examine himself, to ensure that the rebuke was not leading to anger. He always ended with words of praise and friendship or with a gift.

When the yeshiva in Rostov began to develop in a direction he thought improper, Rav Yosef Yozel made a three-day trip by train and, after examining the situation, closed the school. He used to say, "He who hasn't the courage to close a yeshiva is not permitted to open one." He never became discouraged or demoralized, whatever the circumstances.

He did not allow his son, who was a great scholar, to teach in the yeshiva. This son had his own views about Musar and Rav Yosef Yozel feared that this would eventually compromise the effectiveness of his movement. For similar reasons, he removed his son-in-law, Rav Alter Shmulevitz, widely recognized as one of the generation's greatest scholars, from his position as the *Rosh Yeshiva*. Right was right and obviated family considerations.

He was by nature very soft-hearted. He would cry over the story of the destruction of the Temple, as related in the Talmud. He could not bear to see a child spanked and had to leave the house on such occasions. Whenever necessary, however, he was as unyielding as a rock.

He made for himself a tall *shtender* (study stand) that reached to his nose. When he studied late into the night, this forced him to rise up on his toes and thus to remain awake.

He was universally liked and admired. He welcomed all men with a pleasant countenance and was always available to extend a helping hand. If anyone was in need of something, Rav Yosef Yozel would be there first.

Very rarely would Rav Yosef Yozel agree to expel a student. Also, he never refused to accept a student, whatever his past history and reputation may have been. Every night he would review the student list name by name, to see whether there was a need that was not being filled.

He signed the Hebrew letters *Beis-Beis* after his name, as if it was a degree or a title. This stood for *Baal Bitachon*, one who trusts in God. He was renowned for his total reliance on God in all matters.

He never worried or concerned himself with material needs. In the most dire straights he was always full of joy. Rav Yosef Yozel did not allow his family to hoard provisions, as was the common practice in those times.

A man once entered the yeshiva in Mohilev during *Elul*, while the *birzhe* was taking place. The noisy give-and-take and the din discomfited him and he approached the *Rosh Yeshiva* with a sarcastic question: "Is this an insane asylum?" "Quite right," answered Rav Yosef Yozel. "Here people enter insane and leave lucid."

During his days in Zushan, Rav Yozel would seclude himself in a shack deep in the forest. He studied by the light of candles. One night he had no fire with which to light a candle. Trusting that God would provide, he walked out into the forest. Suddenly a man with a lit candle appeared and walked straight into the dwelling. Still without speaking a word, he placed the candle on the table and walked out. Rav Yosef Yozel kept the stump of that miraculous candle in his house for twenty-two years, as a palpable illustration of what *Bitachon* can accomplish. It was finally lost with all his possessions in a fire. He would say that after that miraculous occurrence he never needed another proof as to the efficacy of *Bitachon*. Many years later, Rav Yakov Konievsky, the Steipler Rav, wrote a poem about this incident.

Rav Yosef Yozel and his student Rabbi Yoel Baranchik planned to spend a night in that shack in Zushan. When they arrived, however, they could not find any mattresses. Rav Yosef Yozel told his student that *Hashem* would surely provide for them. Towards nightfall, Rav Yosef Yozel suggested that they take a walk along the road that ran through the forest. Suddenly a peasant came along with a wagon full of straw mattresses that he had been unable to sell at the local fair. They stopped him but he quoted them a very high price. Rav Yosef Yozel was unwilling to spend that much of the yeshiva's money and the two turned back empty-handed. After some time, the peasant returned and agreed to a lower price. Noting that his student was visibly affected by this turn of events, Rav Yozel stretched his hands to Heaven and cried out, "Look, Yoel. Time will come when each one of us will be asked why this moon did not shine with the brightness of the midday sun" (compare Isaiah 30:26). As he spoke, he began to cry bitterly.

In his youth, Rav Yosef Yozel joined a Musar group that put a special emphasis on living with *Bitachon*. The members of this holy company resolved that none of them would make any decision that might appear to contradict this principle, except with the consent of all the other members. One fellow demurred and refused to be bound in this way, for he had grown daughters and needed to apply his efforts to marry them off. As it turned out, all eventually made good matches for their children—except for that one man.

A householder asked Rav Yozel in jest, "If I decide to study Torah full-time, who will provide my sustenance? Will they throw it down from

Heaven?" "Yes, yes,," he answered, "every day they throw it down from Heaven, only there is no one to catch it and no one to pick it up."

He was told that a certain *tzadik* promised a part of his World-to-Come to anyone who accomplished a particular pressing communal need. One of those present commented that he would also be willing to give up a part of his World-to-Come for such a worthy goal. "But are you willing to give up some of your portion in this world?" came the question from Rav Yosef Yozel.

One Passover Eve his family found themselves completely bereft of provisions. They had no matzo, wine, or food for the coming holiday. Rav Yosef Yozel told his wife that the day was still young and that *Hashem* would surely provide. He went out to the street and was approached by a trustee of a charity foundation, who made an offer to arrange for all of the Rav's Passover needs.

When Rav Yosef Yozel went to Odessa to found a yeshiva, he did not have a penny in his pocket. Nevertheless, with nary a concern, he took a room at a local hotel and went to work on this project. He succeeded but it was not until much later that he was able to repay the debts that he incurred in the process.

He was once asked: "Why does one need Musar? We have the *Shulchan Aruch*, isn't that enough?" He answered, "The very first law of the *Shulchan Aruch* is that one should not be frightened of those who scoff at his Divine Service. So without Musar one can't even start the *Shulchan Aruch*."

After his marriage to Rav Yosef Yozel's daughter, Rav Avrohom Jofen began to deliver lectures in the yeshiva. On one or two occasions he was unable to do this. His father-in-law then told Rav Jofen that this concerned him. "I permitted myself to pay for the wedding with the yeshiva funds because there was a benefit for the yeshiva. If you miss on delivering your lectures, a doubt arises regarding this reasoning."

He never turned away a student because the yeshiva lacked funds or because he had not been enrolled in a yeshiva previously. He would say, "Each student comes with his own portion" (*Niddah* 31a). By this he meant that the yeshiva's income is determined by its needs, not its fiscal reserves. He borrowed extensively for the yeshiva and was always in debt. One of his lenders related that at one time Rav Yosef Yozel owed 400 rubles. When the creditor came to collect, Rav Yosef Yozel not only did not appear concerned, but actually asked for another loan. The *Rosh Yeshiva*'s sincerity so impressed this businessman that he lent the yeshiva another large sum of money.

When the famed supporter of Torah study and philanthropist Ovadia Lachman passed away, many yeshivas sent representatives to the administrators of his estate to represent their interests in the division of the estate. Rav Yosef Yozel also went, but midway there he reconsidered. He felt that this might not be consistent with the quality of *Bitachon* and returned home.

Rav Meir Atlas asked a certain philanthropist, "Why do you give my school five rubles, while for Novarodok you provide all that they ask?" He replied: "When Rav Yosef Yozel comes in, he walks right into my living room and spreads himself all over my precious sofas and covers. His attitude negates my wealth and status and tells me that were it not for charity my riches would be worthless. At that time I do not feel the importance of money and I am able to provide generously. You, on the other hand, come in so respectfully and gently and you wait in the hallway until my servants call you in. You are considerate of the furnishings and decor and treat me with great deference. My money rises in value in my own eyes and I can only give you this much."

Rav Yosef Yozel approached a certain well-known philanthropist for a donation. As was his wont on such occasions, he spoke of purifying one's character traits. As he talked of these exalted matters, Rav

Yozel was transported into higher spheres. The philanthropist was also moved and thrust a large donation into Rav Yozel's hands. The Rav was rudely jerked back to the mundane world. Amazed at the man's temerity and totally oblivious of the initial purpose of his visit, he cried out, "See, here. If you ever want to cross my threshold again, take away these despicable things."

The administration of the yeshivas voted to dismiss several students whose involvement in the secular and revolutionary movements was causing much harm. Rav Yosef Yozel ordered that they be given sufficient money for their initial needs upon discharge. One of the administrators objected on the grounds that these individuals were liable to cause more harm to the yeshiva with these funds. Rav Yosef Yozel responded, "Their dismissal is in itself a great affront and indignity. It is not proper to add financial ruin to it as well."

While staying in an inn he entered into an argument with a *Maskil*. The man obstinately defended his point of view. In the middle of the conversation, the *Maskil* motioned to his servant to harness the horses and to prepare to continue on his way. Rav Yosef immediately broke off the discussion. The *Maskil* was surprised at this abrupt end to their conversation. Rav Yosef explained to him that he never argued and disputed something for the sake of verbal logistics and intellectual exercise alone. A debate must serve a practical purpose. "If we dispute and try to find the truth, how can you order your servant to continue to wherever you originally planned to travel? Is it not possible that as a result of our conversation you might turn from your previous path onto a different direction? This proves that you are already set in your ways and that you do not really seek the truth. You want to spend some time in interesting conversation; this is not my way."

He used to say: "When you argue with a freethinker, always try to be the one to offer the last argument. Otherwise, some of his views may rub off and remain with you."

He once said to a *Maskil*: "You think that you are a heretic. If I agreed, it would be forbidden for me to speak with you. I will show you, however, that you are only a man with desires."

A group of students from a secular Jewish school turned to Rav Yosef Yozel with a request to explain his views to them. He told them that they must first agree to join his yeshiva for at least a month. "As long as you are tied to your physical desires," he said, "you will never be able to see things from a spiritual point of view."

Rav Isser Zalman Meltser of Slutsk was asked, "Why is it that Yosef Yozel has not written any significant works of talmudic scholarship?" He responded, "The self-sacrifice, the boundless trust in God, and Rav Yosef Yozel's transcendence of the self—these are his writings."

A "modern" yeshiva was opened in Novarodok. In this institution, Torah and secular knowledge were to be combined and studied. Rav Yosef Yozel kept a close watch over the school and endeavored to influence its students. A Rav of a small town wrote that his son had left home to enter the new school. "My son," he explained, "has tasted of the Tree of Life and now also wishes to partake of the Tree of Knowledge." The students of Novarodok met the child and brought him to Rav Yozel. This is what he told the boy:

> True, you have come to taste of the Tree of Knowledge. Know, however, that the end will be as it says, ". . . and their eyes opened and they knew that they were naked" (Genesis 3:7). Eventually, you will ask yourself that penetrating question: "Where am I? Yesterday I could see from one end of the world to the other (*Genesis Rabbah* 19,17). Now it is only 'in the garden.'" Human wisdom is nearsighted; it sees only into the garden of self-love and notices only what man's heart desires. But the Torah gives a man the sight of an eagle to see all the immeasurable consequences of every deed. Understand then, what you choose for yourself.

The young man was deeply moved. He joined Rav Yosef Yozel and developed into one of the greatest leaders of the Novarodok movement, Rabbi Yitzhak Elchonon Valdshein.

Rav Yosef Yozel was invited to a meeting in the house of a major supporter of the yeshiva, a man who contributed a vast sum of three to four thousand rubles every year. This meeting was ostensibly to discuss an increase in this allocation. Those who accompanied him, as the Novarodok delegation, wanted to hire a coach for the sake of the yeshiva's prestige but the *Rosh Yeshiva* demurred, saying that he did not wish to spend the yeshiva's money for such a trivial purpose. When they entered the philanthropist's home, the latter began to inquire about the educational methods in the yeshiva. It became clear that he expected to approve of these if his allocation was to be increased. Rav Yosef Yozel then informed him that the educational system in the yeshiva was solely under the *Rosh Yeshiva*'s jurisdiction and that the money could come just as well from another source. They left the house, and the delegation was amazed to see Rav Yosef Yozel call for a coach. "On the way here," they said, "when you expected an increased endowment, the coach was too expensive. Now, it no longer is?" Rav Yosef Yozel replied, "Before, the money had to come out of the yeshiva's account. Now it is from the account of the Master of the World and there is no reason to stint on that." When the philanthropist heard of this, he was impressed and did, in fact, markedly increase his annual contributions.

Every Yom Kippur Eve, Rav Yosef Yozel would take extended leave from his family. He would say, "We now go to stand in judgment and who knows how we will come out of it."

He bought a lottery ticket. In his *Bitachon*, he was certain that he would win and made a distribution plan to include the many needs of the Jewish communities in Russia. These plans were discovered years later and were found not to include any disbursement for Rav Yosef Yozel himself or his family. He did not win, however.

The Ukraine and Belarus were in turmoil. A number of factions fought each other and each one abused and terrorized the citizens.

On many occasions they pillaged and murdered people in the towns that came under their control. In fear, people hid in their basements. Rav Yosef Yozel, however, would go about his business as if nothing were wrong. His schedule did not change one iota and he would walk to the *mikva* or the study hall as usual. On one occasion he took along a student. Suddenly rifle fire was heard and a man next to them fell down dead. The student fainted from fright. Rav Yosef Yozel, however, was completely unaffected. On another occasion, during *Havdalah*, a group of ruffians burst into the courtyard of his home, accompanied by wild screams and gunfire. He did not flinch and continued the ceremony as if nothing had happened. Not one drop of wine was spilled.

Rav Yosef Yozel traveled to Charkov with a group of students. Midway to their destination they were taken off the train by the dreaded Cheka, the secret police, and were jailed. Under the conditions of the time, shooting suspected counterrevolutionaries was easier than uncorking a flask of vodka. The boys trembled with fear. Rav Yosef Yozel sharply rebuked them, insisting that the soldiers had no power to hurt them. He ordered them to start up a discussion on the subject of *Bitachon*. As usual, with this type of Musar study there was much commotion and heartfelt crying. Their captors, seeing intense and frenetic activity under these circumstances, were astonished and thought the students to be frankly insane. They therefore released them to continue on their way.

When the Communists put up posters prohibiting Torah study under the penalty of death, Rav Yozel was approached by several worried students. "Why do you read posters?" he questioned them. "Your job is to spread Torah."

He came to Berdichev to found a yeshiva. Shortly before his visit, the Cossacks carried out a major pogrom. Rav Yozel was not deterred. That same day the Berdichev yeshiva was set up and began to function.

In his youth Rav Yosef Yozel made a pact with a friend that the one who died first was obligated to appear to the other one within thirty days of his death and reveal what goes on in the other world, as well as his particular verdict after judgment. Many decades later the other man passed away and appeared to Rav Yosef Yozel while he was putting on *tefillin*. Rav Yosef Yozel waved him away and later commented, "We know all that we need to know from our Sages' words; why do we need any more proofs?"

In Novarodok, people who led a comfortable spiritual life and were satisfied with common conceptions, were referred to as *baalei batim*, householders. Rav Yosef Yozel said that it is preferable to err spiritually than to be a *baal bais*. One who makes mistakes at least has some hope of finding the proper path. The *baal bais* is secure in his way and will never change. One must always strive higher and higher.

Novarodok distrusted simple faith. Man's inclination is shrewd and can easily confuse those who are not trained in Musar thinking and spiritual wisdom. Rav Yosef Yozel offered a parable to illustrate this point.

> There was once a king who sent his minister on a mission and commanded him not to gamble, under any circumstances. During his trip, he met a man who mocked this dignitary for being a hunchback. The latter was, of course, deeply offended by this patently untrue accusation. The man then bet him a very large sum of money that indeed he was a hunchback. "Well," reasoned the minister, "here is an easy way to prove my case and make money," and he agreed. When he returned, he discovered that the king had bet a much larger sum that his servant could not be cajoled into a wager.

Without constant analysis and reflection, man can easily be fooled and is liable to remain bereft of any spiritual attainments.

Whenever he was not sure whether to go to a particular place or to undertake a project, he would first arrive and prepare himself and then consider the issues. Otherwise, Rav Yosef Yozel was concerned that natural human inertia and laziness would affect his judgment. After effort had already been expended, however, a person could think clearly.

During a particularly difficult period in Kiev, he thought of moving the yeshiva to Gomel. He worried, though, that his decision might be influenced by a desire for more comfortable accommodations. To obviate this, he rented a room at a fancy hotel while he pondered the move.

When World War I broke out, some felt that the yeshiva should remain in Novarodok in order to fall into German hands. At that time the German Army was much more fair and evenhanded towards the Jewish population than the Czar's forces. Rav Yosef Yozel did not agree. He felt that German occupation, with its "enlightenment," was spiritually dangerous; thus he chose to move deeper into Russia instead.

A *Rosh Yeshiva* whose school was doing poorly once visited him in Gomel. Uncharacteristically, Rav Yosef Yozel began to complain of his difficulties and lack of success. Afterwards, he explained that he did this precisely in order to spare his visitor's feelings regarding the great success of Novarodok.

One time his wagon driver lost his way and Rav Yosef Yozel had to spend *Shabbos* in the home of a village Jew. It turned out that his host had grievances against a deceased benefactor of Musar. Rav Yosef Yozel applied great effort to convince the villager to forgive this man and eventually succeeded. "See how great is the *mitzvah* of benefiting the public," he said to his students. "Heaven brought me here expressly for the purpose of obtaining forgiveness for the soul of the departed."

Sometimes, in making decisions, he would determine where his inclinations led him and then do the opposite.

During the war years, he was caught in a train compartment surrounded by soldiers who were searching for contraband. All the other passengers were terrified. In order to remove fear from himself, he went over to one of the soldiers and engaged him in conversation. He then read the *Shema* loudly and with great concentration to impress upon himself an awareness of God's sovereignty and that before Him all the soldiers and all the policemen are as nothing.

On the eve of Yom Kippur, Rav Yitzhok Orlansky found his teacher looking depressed and tearful. Rav Yozel raised his eyes to him and said bitterly, "Today we said *selichos* and we said, 'How can I raise my face to the One who cannot be bribed?' I am devastated. For months now, I have been trying to find ways of bribing Him . . . with small amounts . . . now the bitter truth is thrust in my face. Be gone! The door is closed to those who give bribes."

He was full of worldly wisdom. This enabled him to affect each person in the specific ways that were required to attract him to the study of Musar and Fear of Heaven.

A quote from a former student:

> He was a wonder of a man, happy and glad and joyful. Everything about him was Life, every motion of his body joy and gladness like that of a teenager. He was sixty at the time. And the eyes—I will never forget those eyes. They changed colors and expressions, passing from one emotional state to another, all reflected on a wise and understanding face. You felt that here was a man who ruled completely over every limb of his body and who could command it to do whatever he pleased. His will was awe-inspiring, focused, and centered, the will of a man free from all psychological baggage. One sensed a strong personality that cast a spell on all who came close.
>
> I remember our first conversation. We walked along the main street of the town. He didn't speak to me at all about spiritual matters. He asked me whether there was a trolley in Minsk, and other such things. Yet amidst all this he managed to insert psychological observations,

wise insights that, like posthypnotic suggestion's, remained within and could not be driven out.

I remember that a boy and girl, linked arm-in-arm and merrily laughing, passed us by. He grasped my arm and said this to me: "You think that these people are happy? My precious one, they have bundles of troubles. I know this even though I don't know them. All their mirth is to fool others and to fool themselves. When you grow older, you will understand this. I have known only one man who was truly happy—this was Rav Yisroel Salanter."

A quote from another student, who left the Torah fold but never forgot Novarodok:

Not everyone internalized these things; many of us, despite everything, did not achieve what Novarodok and Rav Yosef Yozel wanted. We couldn't give up the world. You might say that Musar did not help us.

Yet there isn't one of us, wherever he might be today, in the farthest walks of life or in its deepest depths, who, even after the passage of decades and decades, does not at times awaken in the middle of the night and once again yearn to learn Musar.

So, we lost ourselves and we let the reins of our lives slip away. Yet we still hold on, from far away, to a weak, worn-out thread. Yes, we wound up in the marsh but we have not sunk there. Yes, we have worshiped idols but we did not bow down to them. Yes, we compromised with our longings but we did not sate them. Sin has ruled us for days, months, years—but Musar still holds us, Musar does not let us go.

These many years we have not even held a prayer book in our hands, these many years Jewish thoughts have not arisen in our minds. We have not pronounced the word "God," or even the word "pure." Yet suddenly, and despite ourselves, we are standing in a corner of the room and we cry and bellow. All the culture and fine education slips away. All the enlightenment disappears. We know once again that we are Jews and that, woe, we are common and vulgar and empty. Friend, where haven't we met? Brother, we have not been utterly lost. In any place to which we may come, there we are still enveloped in the *Mesilas Yeshorim*.

# 16
# The Sayings of Rav Yosef Yozel

If you missed your train, do not say, "I came late and missed my train." Say, rather, "I came too early for the next train—for everything is in the hands of Heaven" (*Berakhos* 33b).

---

He said, "I have never concerned myself whether I can do something but only whether it has to be done. If it must be done, with God's help, one will be able to accomplish it."

---

The sons of Ches called Avraham "My master"(Genesis 23) many times but he never called them the same in return. Even though Avraham bowed down to them, to him there was no Master but God.

---

"And I cleared out the house." Rashi explained—from idolatry (Genesis 24:31). For money, Lavan will even dispose of his gods.

If you are a true *Baal Bitachon*, then you are truly wealthy. If you are only thought of as *Baal Bitachon*, then you are only thought to be wealthy.

---

He who learns Torah only to satisfy his own needs is like a snake, which may eat all the finest delicacies in the world but which perceives in them only the taste of dust and never recognizes that there is something higher than that (*Yoma* 75a).

---

He who wants to compete with and to overcome his friend has already been overcome by his own self. In the end he will also be overcome by his friend.

---

The poorest and most meager present is superior to and more valuable than the most promising future.

---

Man wants to achieve greatness overnight and he wants to sleep well that night, too.

---

Man uses his wondrous intellect for physical gains. Instead of reaching for the supernal spiritual light with it, he hitches it up to chase a piece of bread. This is like the villager who finds a remarkable sculpture wrought by a great master and, in his boorishness, thinks it perfect to serve as a scarecrow in his little garden and to frighten away wild birds from his seedlings.

---

The Midrash relates a story about two birds that fought bitterly until one of them killed the other. The bird that remained then brought a certain herb and revived its dead friend. A man passed by and witnessed this. Said he to himself, "Since this herb revives the dead, let me use it and become rich." He took it and ran joyfully to the city. On the way he saw a carcass of a dead lion and thought to himself, "Let me test this herb to see whether it still has its powers." He placed it upon the lion. The lion rose up and devoured that man.

So it is with this world. A person has the power to enliven and awaken the good in himself, to enshrine and set his intellect to rule over all his desires. What does he do instead? He uses this ability to subjugate himself even more to his lower instincts . . . like that person who brought the raging lion to life and was consumed by it.

---

Repentance is the most profitable business in the world, for it is the only one which turns liabilities into assets.

---

Once upon a time, it was true that "no man sins if not that a spirit of folly enters him" (*Sotah* 3a). Today, no man performs a good deed if not that a spirit of purity enters him.

---

The worth of a yeshiva is determined not by how many good or bad students it has but by what it calls good and by what it calls bad.

The worst thing that can happen to a person is to remain asleep and untamed.

---

"Who shall go up to the mountain of God and who shall persist in his Holy place?" (Psalms 24:3). Although one must constantly strive to rise higher and higher, one must also labor to preserve the gains of the past.

---

It says of Yosef that he mocked and belittled his inclination to sin (*Sotah* 43a). When the reasoning "How can I do this evil thing and sin to God" (Genesis 39:9) did not work, he repeatedly explained and demonstrated to himself how petty his lust was. We must also do the same. One can avoid sin by cutting it down to size, just as surely as by raising oneself above it.

---

There was once a provincial duke who became a king and commissioned a famous artist to decorate his new palace. The man was world-renowned and, as the work progressed, everyone was awed and inspired by the beauty that was taking shape. The artist, however, appeared to grow more and more sullen and unhappy. Finally he ordered the workers to tear down the structure and to start again from scratch. They asked him, "Why do you destroy a thing of such beauty?" "To you," he replied, "this may be a true marvel, but I am an expert in these matters and I know otherwise."

Only the man himself can know what he is missing.

The degree of enthusiasm in prayer reveals the level of one's *Musar*.

---

A person often allows his mind to become an open inn. People and ideas come and go, leaving behind thoughts and impressions, while the owner stands there at the door in astonishment and does not know his own soul.

---

The feeling and the emotion that one experiences during Musar study is like a momentary flash of lightning. In a moment it passes—but this is enough to help a traveler to find his way through the darkness.

---

Man is like a fly that falls into a lit kerosene lamp. There is fire at the wide bottom of the flask. The fly rushes away, upward, but is singed by the hot air that accumulates at the narrow upper neck of the vessel. Bewildered, it reverses course to be consumed by the fire below. The fly does not realize that to push past the hot air is to escape. Man has intelligence but still acts in the same mindless manner. At the moment of trial, he is caught between the fire of his desires and the pain of giving up that which he wants. If he only persevered, the pain would last but for a moment and then he would be free.

---

Utensils can be dairy, fleishig, or parve but a man cannot be parve—only this way or the other.

That which cannot leaven is not usable for matzo (*Pesachim* 35a). He who is not of this world is not fitting for Heaven, either.

---

He who has nothing of this world, has nought in the World-to-Come.[1]

---

He who cannot buy kindling without being cheated lacks also in Musar and Fear of Heaven.

---

One must accustom oneself not to reflect on other people at any time except when one considers how best to benefit them.

---

If the foundation is bent, all that is built upon it comes out twisted, too.

---

God-fearing people investigate every action to see whether it is forbidden. Others examine every matter to see whether it is permitted.

---

1. Only a man of faith can enjoy this world. The others chase anxiously and with no satisfaction after its illusory benefits. The more they drink of its riches the thirstier they become. One who truly enjoys this world can be presumed to have reached a high spiritual level.

"Once upon a time, there was a farmer who had a puppy and a horse. He treated the puppy as one would treat a child. The puppy ate out of his master's bowl and slept in his bed and was showered with attention. The horse labored day and night. The frost bit it during the night and heat afflicted it by day. It slept in a narrow stall and ate but straw and dried grass. "Why should the little dog have it so good?" the horse often wondered. "How does he serve our master better than I?

One evening the horse peeked through the barn window and saw the puppy jumping all over the peasant. It licked his face and nuzzled his hair and the farmer was obviously greatly pleased. "This is what I must also do," concluded the horse. With effort it broke out of the barn, bounded into the house, and began to pummel its master with its great big hoofs.

The Master of the World does not want horseheads.

---

Even the rich have only one stomach and can only eat one meal at a time.

---

I wonder how a man can dare to allow these words out of his mouth: "This is mine."

---

We must sow everywhere, but pay special attention to where it sprouts.

---

To accomplish anything, a man must "stick it"—to the world, to his family, and to himself. This last is the hardest.

In wartime, even an ordinary soldier can become a general.

---

The accepted wisdom is that worldly people have this world, while the people of Torah have the World-to-Come. He who learns Musar knows that the worldly do not have this world and that the Torah scholars should worry about whether they really do have the World-to-Come.

---

Even a thief, in an argument, calls his antagonist a thief.

---

Simple piety, by itself, can not protect from the powers of nature.

---

The world is like a fancy restaurant. He who sits at a table and awaits his order will be nicely served and pampered. A person who rushes to the kitchen to get his food will have to serve himself. He who trusts in God will obtain all his needs with ease and comfort. He who doesn't, labors and wears himself out all his days.

---

He who fails and concludes from that he must change his whole religious philosophy is like a man whose lock was broken open by thieves. Will he move into another dwelling? Surely he will simply put a stronger lock on his door.

One who is on the deck of a moving ship and decides to return to the port cannot get there by walking toward shore. So, too, a man cannot improve himself while in bad company.

---

He who works to correct only his actions and does not repair the flaws of his soul is like the midget who woke up one night and joyfully cried out that he had grown. He concluded this from the fact that usually his feet did not reach the foot of the bed and now they do. His friend turned on the light and found him stretched out across the width of his bed.

---

A person decides to be careful in a particular matter in which he tends to fail. Soon, however, the situation occurs again, but a little differently, and he fails again. He is like the village fool who practical jokers talked into walking down the main street with a sack over his head. Some kind people saved him and explained to him that he should not consent to such pranks again. Soon he was seen walking down the street with a basket on his head. When his benefactors questioned him, he answered, "You told me about the sack but nothing about the basket."

---

The king of Khazars wished to please God. He had a dream in which he was told that his intention was pleasing to God but his actions fell short. This moved him to investigate the religions of the world and he came to recognize the superiority of Judaism.

We also long to find the true way; why then aren't we also favored with dreams to guide us?

The difference is that the king of Khazars was determined to act immediately upon the truth that would be revealed to him. We already know what we must do and we don't even follow that. God does not intervene in the natural world in order to add to our store of abstract knowledge.

---

You must know that the world was created according to the Torah. If the Torah says something, it must be exactly so. Rabbi Yochanon Ben Zakkai put his life in danger when he hailed the general Vespasian as the king (*Gittin* 56b). He could have been put to death for this. Was he not afraid to risk all his diplomacy by saying those unnecessary words? But for Rabbi Yochanon, the Torah indicated that Vespasian was king. The reality simply could not have been any different.

---

A man who tries to practice *Bitachon* while leaving himself a backup plan is like a person who tries to learn how to swim but insists on keeping one foot on the ground.

---

How does the approach of Novarodok differ from that of other Musar schools? All other adherents of Musar pass through the raging sea of life in the same ship as the rest of humanity. When cracks appear in the bottom, they do everything possible to stopper and repair them. The followers of Novarodok, however, jump overboard into the few small lifeboats and face the raging sea alone.

# IV
# *The Next Generation*

# 17
# Rav Avrohom Jofen

Rav Jofen was born near Pinsk and already showed great promise in his childhood. At the age of seventeen the *"Iluy* from Pinsk" became one of the closest disciples of Rav Zalman Sender Shapiro, from whom he learned a deep and penetrating method of talmudic analysis. Sometime in the next several years he met Rav Yosef Yozel and followed him to Novarodok. There he began to deliver lectures that were renowned for depth and accuracy. He married the daughter of Rav Yosef Yozel and absorbed and assimilated his views and ways. Throughout his life he remained faithful to the teachings of Novarodok and strove, through his wide-ranging erudition and dispassionate analysis, to base them on the bedrock of talmudic precedent. After Rav Yosef Yozel's passing, he led the movement in Russia and, subsequently, in Bialistok, Poland. Rav Jofen's dedication to his students was total and it would be correct to say that he had no personal life. The house was always wide open and all of the cupboards and storage places were available to the yeshiva students. During the week, some twenty students ate with Rav Jofen at his table. On *Shabbos* the number was more than twice that. Many boys also slept there. Frequently, they were laid down on the *Rosh Yeshiva*'s bed while he slept on the floor or on doors that were taken off their hinges. His home was a beehive of activity into the early hours of the morning—the nerve center of the Novarodok movement. All of Rav Jofen's existence was dedicated to advancing the spiritual and material well-being of his students. He once defined the essence of Novarodok thusly: "Our way is to place worry for others before concern for ourselves." After the Nazi invasion of Poland, he and many of his students found refuge in Vilna, which was soon afterwards occupied by the Russians. Miraculously, he was able to obtain visas to Japan and from there to the United States.

The first years in America were occupied with rescue activities and in establishing the Beth Joseph in Brooklyn, New York. In this he was assisted by his son Rav Yakov Jofen and sons-in-law Rav Yehuda Leib Nekritz and Rav Chaim Boruch Faskowitz.

In 1965 he moved to Jerusalem, where he founded Beis Midrash Gevoha for Torah and Musar. At 83, he was a wonder to behold—in full possession of his awesome powers and full of energy and enthusiasm.

He passed away on the 13th of *Nissan* 1970, after performing *Bedikas Chometz* for the upcoming Passover holiday.

---

Rabbi Simai taught: "When Israel said 'We shall do' before 'We shall hear,' six hundred thousand angels descended unto each Jew and crowned him with two crowns—one for 'we shall do' and one for 'we shall hear'" (*Shabbos* 89b). The surface understanding of this would be that the two crowns were exactly the same. This is puzzling; after all, the acceptance of the commandments appears to be more praiseworthy than learning about them. You would think that "hearing" is secondary and was mentioned only to contrast and highlight the faithfulness of Israel, who accepted the Torah before learning its contents.

The ways of God are hidden from us. We do not understand the greatness of "hearing." We do not appreciate that, in truth, it is "hearing" which prepares a person to become a vessel worthy of receiving Divine abundance.

"And He led you forty years in the desert . . . and God did not give you the heart to know" (Deuteronomy 29:3).

Rabba said: "From here we derive that a man does not understand his master's view till the passage of forty years" (*Avodah Zarah* 5b). Rav Yisroel Salanter explained that one should not become discouraged if one does not sense inner change, despite the study of Musar (*Or Yisroel* 30,13). How did Rabbi Akiva begin? He was forty years old and had not studied Torah. He was standing at the entrance of a well. He asked: "How did this stone become so worn out?" People answered him, "The water that continuously fell on it wore it away." He immediately reasoned: "If soft water can etch out this hard rock, then the words of Torah, which are as hard as iron, can surely shape my heart, which is merely flesh and blood. Immediately he turned to the study of Torah (*Avos d'Rabbi Noson* 6)."

When Menashe, King of Israel, saw the suffering that had come upon him he said: "I remember that when I was a child, my father made me read this verse: 'In your trouble these things will come upon you at the end of days and you will return unto *Hashem*, your God, and hearken to His voice.'" The angels were then shutting the portals of Heaven before him so that his supplications would not rise. Said the Holy One Blessed Be He to Menashe: "If I do not accept your prayer, I will be closing the door before others who wish to repent." So he made for him a special passageway under the Throne of Glory and accepted his entreaty (*Pesikta d'Rav Kahana* 162).

Do you see the power of "hearing"? Through it, even a great sinner like Menashe was able to return to God in repentance (*Sanhedrin* 101b).

Rabbi Akiva, in his humility, feared that the weight of the many previous years without Torah would prevent him from overcoming his inclinations and conquering his "nature," his long-standing habits. The waters of the well allowed him to "hear" and he immediately turned this lesson into action. We must seize the spark of insight that falls in front of us and advance with it on the way that we must travel.

# 18
# Rav Avrohom Zalmanes

Rav Zalmanes was born in Mir, where his father served in a rabbinic position. From early childhood he dedicated himself to Service of God and to study of Torah. He married Rav Jofen's sister and served as the head of the yeshiva in Rostov. After the yeshiva escaped from Russia, he reestablished it in Warsaw. One of his reasons for choosing this great Jewish city was to be able to learn from the many *tzadikim* and *admorim* of that city. Rav Zalmanes's lack of concern for material things was legendary. He refused to pay heed to any danger or to recognize any power or force that could lead to lessening of Torah study.

He perished in the Warsaw Ghetto in 1944.

---

The basis of Musar is to rethink and examine everything, even that which appears to be completely self-evident. We find in Ethics of the Fathers(4,1) "Who is wise? . . . who is strong? . . ." This inquiry itself teaches us—to investigate, to ask. After we look deeper, we find that things are not as they originally appeared. The truth is in fact often the very opposite of the appearance. A wise person is one who learns from all—not one with scholarly credentials. A strong person is one who conquers his inclination—not one who is a muscle-bound giant.

The foundation of all progress is searching and questioning. That is why this *Mishnah* starts in this manner, with a query. We are taught here a most valuable lesson. Even the simplest thing has in it great depth and profundity. You must search and delve deeply and you will find it. This is the essence of Musar.

# 19
# Rav Dovid Bliacher

Rabbi Bliacher was born in Homan, Russia, where his father was a *shochet*. After studying in Slobodka, he went to Novarodok and became one of the earliest and closest disciples of Rav Yosef Yozel. He was active in setting up yeshivas in Russia and served as head of a yeshiva in Kiev and later in Mezritch. Rabbi Bliacher was also instrumental in founding of the Beis Yosef yeshiva in Bnei Brak.

His dedication to Musar and complete lack of interest in material things was unusual even in that generation. Although he managed to transfer most of his students to Vilna ahead of the Nazi invasion, he himself hid out in a bunker in Mezritch. There he succeeded in eluding capture for over a year. Many stories of his selfless dedication and acts of kindness to his compatriots in hiding have been recorded. He perished in Maidanek. His last act before entering the gas chamber was to organize a *minyan* for *Mincha*, as an act of sanctification of God's name.

---

"After these words, God tested Avraham" (Genesis 22:1). The Sages tell us that Satan said to the Holy One Blessed Be He: "From all these celebrations that Avraham had made [for his son], didn't he have one turtle dove to offer to You as a sacrifice (*Sanhedrin* 89b)?

They also stated that when Avraham took the knife in his hand at the *Akeida*, he wept (*Genesis Rabbah* 56:11). Surely, these were not tears of love for his son, for such love was subsumed into his greater love for the Almighty. Perhaps these were tears occasioned by the realization that all of this could have been avoided, if only he had brought a small sacrifice at the proper time! Still, our father Avraham did not allow feelings of sorrow and regret to vitiate the service that was now to be performed. Now he was to be tested and, whatever its antecedents, here was an opportunity to be uplifted.

We should derive a lesson from this. If trouble comes upon you and you think that it has come as a punishment for a past lapse, do not be filled with guilt and despair. Rather, rejoice in this new opportunity to rise up by the medium of the test that you now face.

The time for contrition is only when it counts. Its purpose is to move you to repentance and to induce you not to return to your folly again. But when you are faced with a test, act, for the repair resides in the wholeheartedness of the deed.

# 20
# Rav Dovid Budnik

Rabbi Dovid Budnik was born in Knishin, Lithuania. In his youth he studied in the Chofets Chaim's yeshiva in Radun where he was influenced by his uncle, Rav Moshe Landinsky, the *Mashgiach* of that yeshiva. His manifold abilities were noted by the *Maskilim*, who mounted a concerted effort to win this promising young scholar to their cause. To escape their blandishments and to strengthen himself against their influence, he traveled to Novarodok. The talents of the newcomer were quickly recognized and Rabbi Budnik became a member of the inner circle of Rav Yosef Yozel's disciples. In a fairly short period of time, he absorbed the spirit of Novarodok and derived therein many new profound philosophical insights. These imbued his fiery Musar discourses with unique character, attracting a loyal following. During the war years, Rav Yosef Yozel sent him to set up yeshivas in Nizni-Novgorod, Mohilev, and Zhitomir. Subsequently Rav Budnik reestablished the yeshiva in Novarodok. When he heard that there were few yeshivas in Latvia, he established there a network of advanced and elementary schools, centered around Dvinsk.

He was murdered by the Nazis, together with all the students of these yeshivas, in 1941. May God avenge their blood.

Four entered the "Paradise," the upper spiritual realm. Ben Azai peeked and died ... Ben Zoma peeked and went mad ... Acher cut down the seedlings (i.e., became a heretic) ... Rabbi Akiva entered in peace and exited in peace (*Chagigah* 14b).

There are four ways of reaching for Heaven.

The first way: A person desires with his whole heart to raise himself up to the greatness of possessing the knowledge of Torah and spiritual perfection. He longs intensely for this goal but it appears so distant that he does not proceed, and eventually he dies from frustration and heartbreak.

The second way: A person is tormented by the recognition of his lowly spiritual state but, because of personal shortcomings or spiritual impediments, finds himself unable to make progress. Having seen the absolute, he cannot accept himself as he is and goes mad. Of this, it says: "And you will go mad from what you see with your eyes" (Deuteronomy 28:34).

The third way: A person blames others for his lack of progress. He feels that he has no friends who understand him and that others do not help him; this makes him feel like an extra wheel on a wagon. On the highest rungs of the ladder that leads upward to Heaven, there is no space for him. Eventually, he becomes angry at God Himself, and also at His servants, for, in his view, they have all led him astray. Because of them, he expended his years in useless struggle, from which he has gained nothing. He rebels and leads others to sin.

The fourth way is that of Rabbi Akiva. Why did he succeed? Rabbi Akiva started on his path inspired by the example of water that, drop by drop, wore away hard rock. He started with the commitment that every step on this way be in truth (translator's note: Rabbi Akiva said: "When you reach the place of white marble, do not call it 'water, water,' for it says 'he who speaks falsehood shall not be established before My eyes'" (*Chagigah* 14b).[1] He sought elevation in the only way

---

1. Also note how this motif recurs in the story related in the same source regarding the error of Ben Zoma concerning the estimation of the distance between the upper and lower waters.

by which one can succeed—the way of truth. He recognized the long and difficult path that lay ahead of him and embarked upon it without hesitation and in truth.

Everything depends on how you start out on your way (*Tosefos Chagigah* 15a).

# 21

# Rav Yisroel Yakov Lubchansky

Rav Lubchansky was born in Baranovich, where his father served as town rabbi. He came to Novarodok soon after the founding of the yeshiva and developed there into a wondrous person. In time he married Feiga Malka, the daughter of Rav Yosef Yozel. After Rav Lubchansky's father passed away, he inherited the rabbinate of Baranovich, where he was greatly beloved for his humility and his dedication to the welfare of the town's inhabitants. Rav Lubchansky, however, felt his calling to be spreading the study of Torah and so, after several years, he gave up the rabbinate and became the *Rosh Yeshiva* of Novarodok schools in Tsaritsin and Charkov. After the movement relocated to Poland, he returned to Baranovich to serve as the *Mashgiach* in Rav Elchonon Wasserman's yeshiva. His piety was renowned; when a student from Baranovich came to the Chofetz Chaim for a blessing, he would say, "You have Rav Yisroel Yakov in your town and you come to me?" It was said that a thick Musar book could be written based on his daily conduct alone.

He perished in the indescribable slaughter in Kovno in the summer of 1941, along with the rest of the Kovno Jewish community.

"Now let Pharaoh search out an understanding and wise man . . . and appoint officers over the land, and take a fifth of the produce of the land in the seven years of plenty" (Genesis 41:33).

This advice appears to be simple logic. Once the facts of the coming famine were revealed, surely it was obvious to all that preparations ought to be made for the future. Is an understanding and wise man the only kind of man that can accomplish this task?

What we have here, however, was a unique kind of challenge. What it now required was preparation for a time which is completely unlike the present. A poor person worries about the future because he senses only too well the precariousness of his situation. Not so the one who is blessed with everything. For him to deprive himself today for the sake of tommorow is very difficult. There are countries where thousands of tons of food are wasted daily with no concern for the future. In prosperity, they don't worry about a possible shortage at some later time.

So it was in Pharaoh's Egypt. Yosef foresaw that during the seven years of plenty, when year after year they harvested an enormous excess of produce, the people would not sense the coming deprivation, would not till the land faithfully, and would not fill the granaries.

For this, a wise and understanding man was needed—to awaken the nation to the dangers of the coming famine. The word *chimesh*, to "take a fifth," Rashi translates as *Veyazrizun*, which means "to encourage." They needed a person who could make people feel the coming danger in their very bones. Similarly, the Sages say, "Who is wise? He who sees what's coming" (*Avos* 4,1). The events of the future must be seen as if they are in front of us, right here and now.

A man must face his spiritual pursuits in exactly the same fashion. Our days are limited in this earthly abode and afterward there comes darkness. That which has not been prepared here will be missed in the hereafter and cannot be made up. "The world is compared to Sabbath Eve and the World-to-Come to Sabbath. If one did not labor on the Eve of the Sabbath, what would one eat on Sabbath? The world is compared to the shore and the World-to-Come to the sea. He who did not prepare on the shore, what would he have when at sea?" (*Ecclesiastes Rabbah* 1,32). In this world, the Torah and its commandments are at your very feet and are available at no charge. Often a man steps over them on his way to some "more important" affair. He thinks that there is still plenty of time; there will be another opportunity to pick up these treasures later.

A man of wisdom and understanding knows that at the future feast "these and those are seated. These eat, but those hunger, these drink, but those thirst" (*Shabbos* 153a). It is told that the Vilna Gaon wept on his deathbed and said, "How precious is this world. Here, for a few pennies, one can fulfill the *mitzvah* of *tsitsis*, in the merit of which he will see the Divine presence." This is the wise man who sees the future.

## 22
# Rav Mordechai Shimanovits

Rav Shimanovits was born in Drevna, near Vilna. His initial education was in the yeshiva of Mir and he came to Novarodok already a formidable scholar. His trust in God, together with his dedication to others, was the bedrock of his being and inspired all of his actions. Once he inherited some money and used all of it to hire wagons to transport the yeshiva students from Novarodok to Gomel, preferring to rely for his own needs on God rather than on his inheritance.

Rav Yosef Yozel sent him to develop the yeshiva in Brogachov. In this, he was immensely successful and attracted many students. After Novarodok fled to Poland, he founded a yeshiva in Biala and later a yeshiva in Ostrovtza. His students saw in their teacher not only a scholar and educator but a paradigm of Torah personality, an example, and a role model, and they were extremely attached to him. Many of them later founded yeshivas in the surrounding towns.

When the Nazis captured the town, they murdered most of its Jews. One of the survivors buried their bodies in the Jewish cemetery. It was subsequently discovered that Rav Shimanovits was laid to rest next to the late Ostrovtsa Rebbe and in close proximity to the burial place of the renowned Rabbi Isaac the Great of Ostrovtza.

Of Noach, it is said, "Noach walked with God" (Genesis 6:9). Shortly afterwards, however, we read that he is called "man of the earth" (Genesis 9:20). What accounts for this change in description?

When a person has a choice of performing only one of two *mitzvos*, he is naturally drawn to the one that is easier for him, according to his constitution. We often see that some people find charitable works easier than in-depth study of the Torah, whereas other individuals are drawn more to study. What the Torah asks of us, however, is to choose the more difficult challenge. Noach had to plant different trees to reestablish the horticulture of the world. He chose to plant the vine first because he was drawn to it. Acting in this manner made him into a "man of the earth," an earthly being.

The Midrash points out that, in contrast to Noach, Moshe was first described as an "Egyptian man" and subsequently as " the man of God" (*Genesis Rabbah* 36:6). What caused this transformation?

When the Jews left Egypt, there was also a choice of *mitzvos*. The Holy One commanded: "Borrow each man from his neighbor . . ." (Exodus 11:12). Here was an opportunity to obtain wealth and do a *mitzvah* at the same time. Moshe, however, gave precedence to another *mitzvah*—he busied himself with retrieving and taking along the bones of Joseph. To choose first the more difficult choice lifts one up to the level of "man of God"; to do the opposite is to descend to the depths of the earth.

# 23
# Rav Yoel Baranchik

Rabbi Baranchik was born in Riga, the capital of Latvia, which was later to become the main sphere of his activities. He was extremely close to the Alter of Novarodok. In his youth the young scholar came into some money and opened a business. He generously supported the yeshiva in Novarodok and spent the whole month of *Elul* there. Because of the demands of his occupation, Rav Yoel did not have enough time for Torah study and sought out Rav Yosef Yozel to pour out his soul and to complain to him. Rav Yozel "blessed" his student that he should lose his entire fortune and be enabled to again devote himself to Torah. Within a short time, a fire consumed his entire stock. Rav Baranchik joyfully accepted this development and he henceforth dedicated himself solely to Torah and communal works.

He was known especially for his Fear of Heaven. It was said that one who saw the trembling of Rav Yoel's entire body when he pronounced a blessing or during prayer saw and recognized true Fear of God. At the same time, Rav Baranchik was expert in the ways of the world and had many friends in the Latvian parliament where he was an advocate, representing the Jewish community. He also established a school along the lines of Rav Samson Raphael Hirsch's *Torah Im Derech Eretz* philosophy. This institution saved Latvian Jewry from spiritual annihilation and directed many of its products into Lithuanian yeshivas for advanced study.

He was a renowned orator and was especially sought after as a speaker at large gatherings. He contributed many articles to the Jewish newspapers and his influence was felt throughout the wider Jewish community.

For some time Rav Baranchik served as *Mashgiach* at the yeshiva of Kletsk under the direction of Rabbi Aharon Kotler. Later he was appointed to direct the teachers' seminary in Grodno founded by Rabbi Chaim Ozer Grodzinski.

---

The Sages said: "To the righteous, the Evil Inclination appears as a mountain and to the wicked it seems no more than a strand of hair" (*Sukkah* 52a). Rav Yitshak Blaser explained that a righteous person sees in each seemingly small strand of sin a potential mountain. I would add that, according to our Sages, he who is obligated and fulfills a commandment is greater than he who is not obligated and does it voluntarily (*Kiddushin* 31a). The *Tosefos* explains that a person who is obligated worries and is concerned lest he be unable to properly fulfill his duty. That leads him to be more meticulous in its performance and to accumulate greater merit. We therefore can understand the reason why the Evil Urge appears as big as a mountain to the righteous. For the wicked, there is no struggle. They do not consider themselves to be truly obligated and do not take such matters to heart. For them, the commandments are optional trifles and they give them but little thought. The wicked simply don't care. The same requirement is like a mountain to one because there is inner struggle, and it is of little consequence to the others.

There is no doubt that one cannot reach that which is truly good unless one studies Musar with feeling and with emotional arousal. We must also contemplate the issues of reward and punishment, in order to gain Fear of Heaven. The way of life lies before us and each person is required to say, "When will my deeds match the deeds of my forefathers?" (*Tanna d'Bei Eliahu* 25).

# 24
# Rav Yitzhak Elchonon Valdshein

Rav Valdshein was born in Shershev near Brisk. His father served as the Rav of that town. It is said that in his youth he traveled to the yeshiva of Rav Krukovsky, later the *magid* of Vilna, who also had a yeshiva in Novarodok, and was "seized" by Rav Yosef Yozel's students when he disembarked at the train station. The students brought him to Rav Yosef Yozel, who asked him, "Why have you come to study specifically under the local Rav?" The boy replied, "Because I also want to study Russian." Rav Yosef Yozel then made a deal with the youth— he could study Russian even in his yeshiva but on one condition. He must first spend one month strictly following the program of the yeshiva. Needless to say, after one month the boy no longer had any desire for secular studies.

Rav Valdshein was a deep thinker and a gifted popularizer of his master's teachings. He was an exceptional educator blessed with profound understanding of the motivations and depths of the human soul. He knew what to say to each student, how to motivate him, how to help him rise to new heights of achievement in Torah and *Musar*. He taught in a number of Novarodok yeshivas: Bialistok, Pinsk, Ostrovtsa, Baranovich. His abilities were recognized by Rav Chaim Ozer Grodzinski, who appointed him to lead the Ramelleis yeshiva in Vilna.

He was also instrumental in editing and publishing the *Madreigas Ho'odom* of Rav Yosef Yozel. He was a brother-in-law of Rav Chaim Shmulevits, the *Rosh Yeshiva* of the Mirrer Yeshiva.

At the outbreak of the World War II he escaped to Vilna, where he died just before the Nazi invasion.

---

Of the generation that built the Tower of Bavel, it is said: "And they found a valley . . ." (Genesis 11:2). The Sages comment, "All the nations had gathered to seek out the valley that fits their purpose." Rabbi Nechemiah says, "As for scoffers, he allows them to scoff" (*Genesis Rabbah* 38:8).

One may wonder, why did God allow them to bring their evil plans to fruition? Why did God facilitate finding the valley that later served as the means of their downfall? It appears that God could have kept them from locating this spot and could have avoided the subsequent tragedy. Since He eventually had to intervene anyway, why not intervene sooner rather than later?

Let us understand what led that generation to their bitter end. That valley made their plan possible, for what they feared above all was dispersal, as they said: "lest we will be scattered over the face of the whole earth." Why were they afraid of this? Because they wished to achieve the ultimate expression of their physical natures and inborn characters. They wished to remain together so that they could share evil ways with one another. They attempted to develop and express to the fullest the human potential for all things, good and bad. The Vilna Gaon had stated that each country possesses its own peculiar bad traits. In Germany it is immorality and in Russia, thievery. In Danzig, which is on the border, the evils of both countries proliferate. There is more, however.

The people that built the tower hoped to defeat the teachings of our father Avraham, who publicly taught humanity about God. The Midrash states: "and same words—directed against Avraham, our father. They said of him that he is sterile like a mule" (*Genesis Rabbah* 38,6). If he was sterile, why were they so afraid of him?

But, they reasoned, had Avraham only had a family of his own, perhaps he would not have been as zealous to spread the true faith among the peoples of the world. Seeing that he was without children, however, they became anxious that he would not rest in his labors and that he would make no accommodation with the corruption of their world. They had to unite and pool their strength to oppose him. Rav Nachman of Breslav says that just as the righteous are afflicted by their physical side so, too, do the wicked suffer from their intellects. Just as the righteous find fulfillment in the very difficulty of their task, in overcoming their inclinations, and in molding their physical selves into holy beings, so too do the wicked fight their conscience in order to reassure themselves that their way is proper and right. They must suppress the stirring of reason and goodness in their breasts.

Everyone knew that the way of Avraham required the utmost self-sacrifice in the pursuit of good. To negate his example, his opponents had to dedicate themselves in equal measure to the demanding task of building the tower of Bavel. They wanted the whole world to see the extent of their devotion and sacrifice and thus minimize the impact that Avraham was making.

But did they not realize the emptiness and falsehood behind their dedication and self-sacrifice? Well, this in fact is the nature of idol worship; it is an attempt to shore up a false belief and to demonstrate to the world that what is wrong is really right.

God allowed them to find the valley which they sought because He wanted subsequent generations to learn from their example. They were so many and they were so powerful. They were confronted by one man—Avraham. Yet they mustered such incredible effort to oppose him. We must understand what is required of us in our own struggle for that which is good. We can succeed and emerge victorious, for this battle is within our power and within our abilities.

When the Jews were about to leave Egypt, they were commanded to slaughter the Paschal lamb and to smear its blood upon the lintel and doorposts of their homes. These represent the three forefathers—Avraham, Yitshak, and Yakov (*Exodus Rabbah* 17:3). The people of Israel had barely arisen out of the forty-nine levels of impurity; this now would be their first *mitzvah*. Yet they were already told that they must reach for the ultimate, for the level of their great forefathers. This is the essence of the Novarodok approach. One must reach for the highest rungs, now, without compromises and without intermediate steps.

# 25
# Rav Shraga Magid

Rabbi Shraga Magid was born in the Lithuanian town of Varzhin. The Alter personally supervised his education and growth and soon young Shraga Magid became an accomplished *Baal Musar* and a great scholar. He served as the *Rosh Yeshiva* in Ludomir. He escaped to Vilna when the Germans invaded Poland. There he was arrested by the Soviets and exiled to Siberia. It is thought that he died there of starvation.

---

The Sages tell us that the account of the manner in which the feet of our forefathers' servants were washed is of greater importance than the laws that were given to their descendants. Thus the Torah elaborates on Eliezer's washing of his feet, while the laws of impurity are derived from a mere implication in a verse (*Yalkut Shimoni Genesis* 109).

How can we relate to this? Why does the Torah tell us that Eliezer washed his feet and how is that valuable to us?

Let us remember that Eliezer had a daughter who he thought would be a proper match for Avraham's son, Yitshak (*Yalkut Shimoni Hosea* 12). Thus, he would have been quite happy had Besuel refused his daughter to Yitshak. But Eliezer chose not to follow roundabout ways to this goal; instead he went out with strength to break his own desire to become part of his beloved master's family and destiny. Instead he prayed that Yitshak's match with Rivka succeed. He even refused to taste Besuel's food "until I have spoken my words" (Genesis 24:33). Thus, he chose the path of unquestioning faith and obedience (*Madreigas Ho'odom, Birur Hamidos*). When Eliezer asked that his feet be washed, he acted in the same fashion.

We know that some people quickly form strong opinions of others solely on the basis of their outward appearance. There are those who take a dislike to people who wear a particular apparel or have certain mannerisms. Eliezer was aware of this. He washed his feet in order to remove any possible impediment to the match that his unwashed appearance might create. In thus disregarding his own desire, he was again acting as the faithful servant.

The Torah teaches us something of immense importance here. Eliezer pursued *Shviras Hamidos* to the utmost, in spite of his personal feelings—in fact, *because* of his personal feelings. The Torah was given to purify us and our practice of Divine Service depends on us correcting our faulty character traits.

# 26
# Rav Nisan Bobruisker

Rav Nisan came to Novarodok from the town of Bobruisk. He was a gifted orator and deep thinker with the ability to influence and inspire. He was never seen to show anger and his pleasant disposition endeared him to everyone. His reliance on God was total and unquestioning and figured in a number of miraculous personal experiences. Rav Nisan composed a number of songs that were sung by the Novarodokers, including one set to the tune of a popular revolutionary hymn. He was murdered by the Nazis in Vilna in 1941.

---

"Sin crouches by the entrance" (Genesis 4:7). Rabbi Tanchum said, "There are crafty dogs in Rome who know how to obtain what they want. A dog goes and sits in front a baker and pretends to be sleeping. The baker also falls asleep. The dog then upsets the baker's cart and scatters the breads all over on the ground. Before the baker can gather his loaves, the dog snatches one of them and carries it away" (*Genesis Rabbah* 22,12).

Why was this specific parable selected to illustrate the tricks of the Evil Inclination?

Oftentimes a man who has stumbled and sinned is filled with remorse over his failure. At other times, however, he comes out with pride and satisfaction at his "victory."

For example, a person may be late for work. His Evil Inclination tells him not to put on *tefillin* because he is running late. Of course, he doesn't succumb and does put them on but he hurriedly mumbles the absolute minimum of the required prayers, tears off the precious *mitzvah* and then speeds off. This man rejoices in his supposed victory and he is proud of his righteousness.

Another example: A wealthy man is tempted to keep his store open on *Shabbos*. He resists, but gradually the business begins to close later and later on Friday and to open earlier and earlier on Saturday night. This man is also proud for, he thinks, he has resisted the temptation of his Evil Inclination.

A man argues with a friend. The dispute grows and heats up until sharp words are exchanged. At the last moment, the two individuals draw back from the brink to which they have come. They do not say the insults that could have been said. These ones also take pride in their refinement and the purity of their character.

Similarly, there are those who do not stand up to the wicked but would much rather seek compromises. At the end, they pat themselves on the back for keeping these scoffers from an even greater apostasy through their tolerant attitude and their "ways of peace."

The Evil Urge is a very shrewd tactician and a master warrior. It leaves itself room to withdraw in order to pursue its grand design and to attack again. It is a seasoned negotiator; it demands more than it really wants. Above all, it wants its victims not to feel bad, to think they won, to remain smug and contented, not to regret the losses they have suffered. Then they will not gather strength to resist, to close the breaches, to go on the offensive.

The parable of the Sages is precise. The dog did not want all the breads. All he wanted was one loaf. By upsetting the whole cart, he led the baker to believe that everything was threatened. When only one loaf was lost, the baker felt a tremendous relief. He will not learn from this experience for he does not realize that he has been tricked. Next time the baker will be fooled again.

We can learn from this, each person according to his own level. We must learn not to compromise even as much as a hair's breadth. That is all that the Evil One wants—just a hair's breadth—and this is where the battle lines are drawn.

# Appendix I
# Novarodok Philosophy of History

Rav Yosef Yozel's historiography deserves a closer look, for it serves as the basis of his approach to the issues of the day. Rav Yosef Yozel saw his movement as being completely within the historical tradition of Judaism. As he saw it, since the Revelation at Sinai, the medium through which God's will became known to us progressed through well-defined stages. There was the period of the Revelation itself, the era of prophecy, and the period of the yeshivas. During each era, great men supported and led individuals through the trials of life; ultimately all was predicated on the dedication of the common folk. With the advent of the Enlightenment, the inner mechanisms of the community were corroded and the commitment of individuals diluted by the spirit of compromise. The masses were corrupted and a gulf opened between the world of average men and the carriers and bearers of Torah truth. In time even the latter became demoralized and isolated and many breaches appeared among them. Novarodok was to be the agent of renewal, that is, a return to the exalted standards of the past. New pathways must now be found to reformulate old values and new institutions which are solely dedicated to such a goal must be reestablished.

The way to renewal lies in the revival of our strongholds—the yeshivas. To achieve this, Rav Yosef Yozel argued that a period of retrenchment and reconstitution was absolutely necessary. The yeshivas must first be renewed in a spirit of total commitment, eschewing any compromises. With that accomplished, the light of Torah will go out to the world and its pristine purity will transform it. Musar can provide the program by which this can be accomplished. The redemption of the individual precedes and provides the impetus for the reform of the entire community. We must start with a radical and total commitment to spiritual renewal. First, we must teach renunciation of the values of the world. A seeker of the truth disdains and laughs at the blandishments of a corrupt society. The emphasis has to be on separation from its influence and renunciation of its false promises and tempting illusions. For this, a courageous spirit and willingness to indomitably oppose falsehood is required. Without unshakable trust in the Almighty, nothing important can be accomplished; such trust must be total and with no regard for the consequences. Inner strength can be harnessed through intense intellectual reflection and profound emotional arousal. This cannot be done in isolation but only as part of a group of seekers committed to the same goal—in other words, a yeshiva. In Novarodok, Rav Yosef Yozel Hurvits created such a place. He created a small community designed to form individuals who would revolutionize the world. Novarodok inspired its adherents with a vision of a new kind of greatness. Rav Yosef Yozel's teachings and institutions brought forth men who were not content with pursuing personal righteousness alone. By the hundreds they went out to found yeshivas and to imbue their students with idealistic zeal and courage.

The idea that growth in Musar includes bringing others closer to Torah is already to be found in the writings of Rabbi Yisroel Salanter; in fact, his life was dedicated primarily to communal work. Rav Yosef Yozel of Novarodok, however, molded his Musar into a unified program of action unique amongst Musar leaders. Many of his ideas have become an integral part of the Torah community's worldview in the postwar period. *Madreigas Ho'odom*, the work containing his teachings, represents the only systematic exposition of Musar philosophy and has had a profound influence on Jewish world and thought.

# Appendix II
# The Yeshiva Schedule

The daily schedule of a Novarodok yeshiva during "the days of seclusion," Purim to Passover:

| | |
|---|---|
| *Shacharis*, morning prayer | 8:30 |
| *Musar* study | after prayer for approximately one hour. |
| Breakfast | 10:15–11:00 |
| *Musar* study | 11:00–12:00 |
| Group *Musar* study | 12:00–12:30 |
| Talmud | 12:30–4:30 |
| *Musar* | 4:30–4:45 |
| *Mincha*, afternoon prayer | 4:45–5:15 |
| Dinner | 5:15–6:45 |
| *Musar* | 6:45–7:15 |
| *Musar Chaburah* | 7:15–8:15 |
| *Halacha* Study | 8:15–9:15 |
| Personal study time | 9:15 |

Everyday schedule of the yeshiva in Bialistok:

| | |
|---|---|
| Independent study | 6:00–7:30 |
| *Shacharis*, morning prayer | 7:30 |

| | |
|---|---|
| Talmud | 9:00–2:00 |
| *Musar* and *Mincha* | 2:00–4:00 |
| Talmud | 4:00–9:00 |
| *Musar* | 9:00–9:30 |
| *Birzhe, Maariv* | 9:30–10:15 |
| Supper | 10:15–10:30 |
| Independent Study | 10:30–3:00 |

# Appendix III
# Novarodok Battle Song

This song was composed by Rav Nisan Bobruisker, to the tune of a well-known revolutionary hymn. The students sang it in the streets when other forms of open opposition to the Communist regime became impossible. The Bolsheviks approved, for, through the melody, they heard only their battle cry. The Novarodokers, however, sang of their own revolution—in the world of spirit.

> Like our fathers of yore, when they faced religious persecution,
> If the day has already come and the hour strikes,
> To fulfill what the Torah demands from us all,
> For the Torah, for God, for the Jewish people,
> We are willing to give our flesh and blood,
> Let them comb our hearts with combs of steel,
> Let them whip us with many whips,
> Like our fathers of yore when they faced religious persecution,
> We are not afraid of anything.
>
> If the day has already come and the time has arrived,
> That Satan smothers all things,
> They will prey upon us, saying, "You can live well,"
> Or they will say, "You can roll in honey and fat,"
> The answer is ready for all of us,
> No, we will not abandon the Torah.

Like our fathers of yore when they faced religious persecution,
We will, with pride, with our heads raised.

If the time has come for our spirit once again,
To reestablish this anew in the world,
We say, "It is better for us to be with the Torah in calamity,
Than to lie in filth with the *"free,"*
What is there except the life of Torah?
Just wounds into which salt was poured.
Like our fathers of yore when they faced religious persecution,
We laugh at all these things.

We remember the day the Jewish nation received,
All that it possesses today,
No ox would disturb, no horse would neigh,
And the angels did *shira* not say,
From up high, from the ground, from all directions,
Were the words of *Anochi* declared.
With our fathers of old in that majestic dawn,
We all heard *Anochi* declared.

There will come the day, the exalted hour,
When everything will be understood by all,
In the ways of God—what is good and what is not,
The young and the old will know it,
Jealousy and hatred will be removed,
The Torah will burn like a flame,
And the world will be filled with the knowledge of God,
Just like water covers the sea.

# Glossary

**Admor(im)**  chasidic leaders.
**Alter**  literally, elder. A title of respect reserved for the most prominent Musar leaders.
**Akeida**  binding of Isaac.
**Aliya**  going up; for example, to the Land of Israel.
**Amora**  a later talmudic sage.
**Anochi**  I, the term used at the opening of the Decalogue.
**Arova**  willow branch, a part of the four species on Sukkos.
**Avodah**  labor, has connotations of holy work.
**Avos**  patriarchs.
**Baalei Batim**  householders, undistinguished people.
**Baal Musar**  a person who has mastered how to live and practice Musar.
**Bedikas Chometz**  search for leaven on the Eve of Passover.
**Beis Midrash**  house of study.
**Bima**  a platform on which the Torah is placed during Torah reading.
**Bina**  understanding.
**Birur Hamidos**  purifying character traits.
**Bitachon**  trust and reliance upon God.
**Chavura**  a group, a fellowship—especially when dedicated to study of a common Torah subject.
**Cheder(im)**  traditional Torah grade schools.

**Chesed** kindness.
**Chochom** wise person, a distinguished Torah scholar.
**Dayan** religious judge.
**Derech** way, path.
**Eirev Rav** mixed multitude of converts that left Egypt with the Children of Israel.
**Fleishig** meat dish, must be kept separate from milk dishes.
**Gaon** an outstanding scholar, in modern times applied to the Vilna Gaon.
**Goral** lot.
**Gulag** Soviet system of prisons and labor camps.
**Haftora** the reading from Prophets that follows the Torah reading.
**Haggada** the text recited during Passover Seder.
**Hakafos** processions around the *Bima* on Sukkos.
**Halacha** Jewish religious law. Literally—the walking.
**Hashem** literally, The Name. A form of reverential address to God.
**Haskalah** enlightenment.
**Havdalah** the prayer over wine, candles, and spices that marks the departure of the Sabbath.
**Iluy** genius. Applied to a youth of exceptional ability.
**Khazars** a people that converted to Judaism. The story of this conversion serves as the backdrop of Kuzari, the classical philosophical and religious work by Rabbi Judah Halevi.
**Kollel** a group of married students who are supported by the community.
**Kevod Shemaim** glory of Heaven.
**Lishmo** for the sake of Heaven or for the sake of the subject matter itself.
**Lulav** branch of a palm tree used in the observance of the Sukkos holiday.
**Maariv** evening prayer.
**Mafkir** to give up, to renounce.
**Maggid(im)** preachers who speak on non-Halacha subjects.

**Mashgiach** in a Musar-type yeshiva, a specially appointed person whose function is to teach Musar, supervise students' spiritual development and oversee the general direction of the institution.
**Maskil(im)** followers of Enlightenment philosophies.
**Matzo** unleavened bread eaten on Passover.
**Melamed** a teacher in *cheder*.
**Mikva** ritual bath.
**Middos** character traits and qualities.
**Milchig** milk dishes. Must be kept separate from the meat dishes.
**Mincha** afternoon prayer.
**Minyan** a quorum, required for communal prayer.
**Mishnah** the collection of laws that serve as the basis of the Talmud.
**Mitzvah (Mitzvos)** commandments.
**Mishpatim** laws that have obvious rational explanations.
**NKVD** national committee for state security, secret police.
**Olam** world
**Omek** depth
**Pesach** Passover
**Pikuach Nefesh** danger to life.
**Pilpul** a sophisticated talmudic discourse.
**Poskim** decisors. Works that focus on final formulation of Jewish law.
**Rambam** Maimonides.
**Ramban** Nachmanides.
**Rav** traditional title for rabbi.
**Rebbe** my teacher, a respectful title; used for a leader of a chasidic group.
**Rebbetzin** rabbi's wife.
**Reidel** discussion.
**Responsa** works of Poskim.
**Ribbono shel olam** Master of the World, a means of addressing God.
**Rishon(im)** early medieval commentators on the Talmud.
**Rosh Chodesh** the first day of the Hebrew month. Has a semiholiday status.

**Rosh Hashana** Jewish New Year.
**Rosh Yeshiva** the dean of a yeshiva.
**Rotseach** murderer.
**Selichos** penitential prayer said on fast days and during the days of Awe.
**Shabbos** Sabbath.
**Shacharis** morning prayer.
**Shamas** a caretaker of a synagogue or of a study hall.
**Shema** basic prayer of Judaism that declares the unity of God.
**Shemaim** Heaven.
**Shira** song, specifically the song of Moses.
**Shiur(im)** a lesson in Talmud.
**Shleimus** spiritual completeness.
**Shmuess(en)** Musar talks.
**Shochet** ritual slaughterer.
**Shofar** ram's horn blown on Rosh Hashana.
**Shtender** special rest for large volumes, used during study in yeshivas.
**Shulchan Aruch** Code of Jewish Law.
**Shviras Hamiddos** breaking of character traits.
**Simcha** a joyous occasion.
**Sugya** a self-contained discussion in the Talmud.
**Succah** a makeshift structure used during Succos holiday.
**Succos** Feast of Tabernacles.
**Tallis** fringed four-cornered garment worn by Jewish men.
**Talmid** student.
**Talmud Torah** study of Torah.
**Tanna** sage of the Mishnah.
**Tefillin** phylacteries, used during *shacharis*.
**Tikkun** repair; has Kabbalistic overtones, denoting achieving completion and ultimate purpose.
**Torah Im Derech Eretz** philosophy of combining Torah ideals and secularly derived religious values, when the latter are compatible with the former. Developed by Rabbi Samson Raphael Hirsch in Germany.

**Tosefos** additions. Notes on the Talmud by medieval commentators of Germany and France.
**Tzadik(im)** righteous ones. Often used to refer to chasidic masters.
**Tsitsis** ritual fringes that are worn every day and during prayer.
**Treif** not kosher.
**Vaad** group. In Novarodok used interchangeably with chavura.
**Yetzer** inclination: for example, Yetzer Hora—Evil Inclination.
**Yiras Shemaim** literally, Fear of Heaven. Refers to a serious approach to religious life and strong commitment to worship and avoidance of sin.
**Zocheh** to merit.

# Bibliography

## PRIMARY SOURCE MATERIALS

### In Hebrew

Bruk, Ben Tsion. *Gevilei Aish*. Jerusalem: Tsur Ot, 1980.
 A compilation of published articles and recollections of teachings from the second generation of Novarodok teachers by the *Rosh Yeshiva* of Beis Yosef in Jerusalem.

Hurvitz, Rav Yosef Yozel. *Madreigas Ho'odom*. Jerusalem: Lipa Friedman, 1975.
 The teachings of Rav Yosef Yozel.

Jofen, Avrohom. *Hamusar Vhadaas*. Bnei Brak: Lipa Friedman, 1963.
 A compilation of Musar talks. The second volume contains a short history of Novarodok written by Rav Yehuda L. Nekritz that contains a wealth of detail but also differs in some particulars from other accounts.

Katz, Dov. *Pulmus Hamusar*. Jerusalem: Weiss, 1972.
 Describes the history of the controversy regarding the Musar movement. Contains a very valuable discussion and historical overview of philosophical differences behind the controversy.

---

NOTE: Years of publication of Hebrew works have been approximately translated into dates according to the secular calendar.

Katz, Dov. *Tnuas Hamusar*, Vol. 4. Tel Aviv: Avraham Tsioni, 1962.
A classic history of the Musar movement. This volume deals with Novarodok.
Semiatycki, Shlomo Naftoli Hertz. *Ner Lasher, Tzahar LYosef, Pinkos Hakabbolos Uvaadim Novaradok*. Bnei Brak, 1989.
Shulman, Moshe Gedalya. *Giduley Moshe*. Brooklyn: Moraiah, 1994.
Musar talks by Novarodok rabbis. Includes some rare photographs.
Sursky, A. *Marbitsei Torah U'Musar*. New York: Sentry Press, 1977.
Biography.
Valdshein, Yitshak Elchonon. *Toras Yitshak*. Bnei Brak: Lipa Friedman, 1973.
A compilation of collected Musar talks and letters by one of the greatest Novarodok teachers.
Zaitchik, Chaim Ephraim. *Hameoros Hagdolim*. New York: Balshon Printing and Offset, 1962 (translated as *Sparks of Musar*. New York: Feldheim, 1992).
Aphorisms, stories, and parables from Musar greats that includes material on Novarodok.
Zaritsky, David. *Gesher Tzar*. Bnei Brak: Netsach, 1968.
A two-volume novel dramatizing the early life of Rav Yosef Yozel Hurvits by a prominent thinker and writer associated with Novarodok.

## FOR FURTHER CONSIDERATION

**In English:**

Friedman, Yaakov B. "Evoking the World of Novorhodok." *Yated Ne'mon*, December 2, 1994.
Goldberg, Hillel. *The Fire Within*. Brooklyn: ArtScroll–Mesorah Publications, 1987.
A personal retelling of author's relationship with Musar teachers in the United States and Israel. Contains much fascinating material on Novarodok.

Hurvits, Rav Yosef Yozel. To Lead the Many to Righteousness. Jerusalem: Feldheim, 1972.
A very literal translation of the last chapter of *Madreigas Ho'odom*.
"The Perfection Seekers." *Yated Ne'emon*. Sept. 23, 1993.
A short article about Novarodok.
Perr, Yechiel Yitshok. "Beyond Relevance: Horav Avrohom Jofen." *Jewish Observer* (July 1970): pp. 19–21.
Perr, Yechiel Yitzhok. "Reb Yisroel—Who was he?" *Jewish Observer* (June 1969): pp. 12–14.
Shapiro, Chaim. "The World of Novarodok." *Jewish Observer* (February–March 1977): pp. 31–37; and "Letters to the Editor" in the subsequent issue.
Reminiscences.
Wallach, Shalom Meir. *The Pesach Haggada, With Commentary Culled from Classic Baalei Musar*. Brooklyn: Artscroll–Mesorah Publications, 1989.

**In Hebrew:**

Blaser, Rav Yitzhak. *Ohr Yisroel*. Vilna, 1901.
Basic works of the Musar movement.
Lipkin, Rav Yisroel Salanter. *Igeres Hamusar* (appended to many *Musar* works, including standard editions *Mesilas Yeshorim*). Jerusalem: Eshkol, 1964.
Nekritz, Daniel. *Leiv Arye*. Brooklyn: Fink Graphics, 1992.
A biography and Musar talks of Rabbi Yehuda Leib Nekrits, who was one of the founders of the Beth Joseph in Brooklyn. Contains dozens of historic photographs.
Valdshein, Yitzhak. *Or Hamevakesh*. Bnei Brak, 1964.
Zaitchik, Chaim Ephraim. *Ohr Hanefesh, Ohros Hachaim, Ohr Chodosh, Hamavet Vhachaim, V'ani Tefila, Pri Hoorets, Pri Chaim, Toras Hanefesh*. Bnei Brak: Lipa Friedman; and Brooklyn, NY: Balshon Printing and Offset, 1967–1986.
Musar thoughts on the portion of the week by a Novarodok *Rosh Yeshiva* in Jerusalem.

## TITLES OF OTHER NOVARODOK WORKS OF INTEREST:

Bornshtein, Chaim. *Chalichos Olam*. Tel Aviv, 1961.
Bruk, Ben Tsion. *Hegionei Musar*. New York, 1949.
*Cheshbono Shel Olam*, Jerusalem, 1944.
*Divrei Bina UMusar*, Tel Aviv, 1970.
*Ohr Hamusar*. Journal published by Novarodok movement in Russia and Poland, 1922–1925, 1931, and in Palestine, 1933. *Chayei Musar*, in Poland, 1933–1935. Reprinted in Bnei Brak in 1964.
*Ohr Torah Umusar*, Jerusalem, 1968.
*Ohros Kovets*, 1936.
Vitkind, Hilel. *Musar Hatorah*. Jerusalem, 1963.
*Zachor L'Avraham*. Bnei Brak: Lipa Friedman, 1973.
Zaritsky, Dovid. *Toras Hamusar*. Tel Aviv, 1959.

# Index

Adam, 55–58, 64, 67, 75
   angels vs., 56
Akiva, Rabbi, 146–147
Amalekites, 91
Amsterdam, Rav Naftoli, 5
Angels, 64
   Adam vs., 56
Anger, 57
Asa, King, 88
Ascetism, Novarodok Musar's
   rejection of, xx
Avraham, 59, 60–63, 94, 158–160
   character of, 61
   Noach vs., 63
   and sacrifice of Yitshak, 62–63
   Satan and, 61–62, 143–144

Baranchik, Rav Yoel, 36, 155–156
Bar Yakov, Rabbi Acha, 66
Beans, mourning and, 94
Belarus, 22
Benevolence, 17
Ben Gurion, Nakdimon, 30
Ben Ilai, Rabbi Yehudah, 17

Ben Navat, Yerevoam, 68
Bialistok, 35, 36, 41
*Birzhe*, 15, 16–17
Bitachon, 83–91
   future and, 86
   livelyhood and, 86–89
   nature's bending to, 84–85
   public service and, 90–91
   "soft," 86–87
   types of, 87–88
Blaser, Rav Yitshak, 5, 7, 10
Bliacher, Rav Dovid, 36, 143–144
Bobruisker, Rav Nisan, 39, 163–165
Boldness of spirit, 18
Bolsheviks, yeshivas persecuted by, 28–30
Bronstein, Rabbi Harry, 45
Bruk, Rav Ben-Tsion, 39
Budnik, Rav Dovid, 31, 33, 145–147

Chaim of Volozhiner, Rav, xvi, xvii
Chanuka, 17–18

Character:
  of Avraham, 61
  bad, man's breaking of, 81
  as key to Torah, 50–51
  of Noach, 59–60
  Torah study and, xvi
Charkov, 24, 28
Chava, 55, 56–57, 64
Chavuros, 15–16, 39
  diary discussions in, 40
  weekly meetings of, 40
Cold War, 45
Communists, jews persecuted by, 28–31, 34–35
Compromise, 79–81

David, 68, 83
Denikin, General, 30
Doing, hearing and, 64

Eisav:
  sale of birthright by, 93–95
  Yitshak's blessing and, 93–97
Eiver, 64
Eliahu, 71
Elul, 16, 18, 40
England, yeshiva founded in, 36
Enlightenment, 37
  Torah and, 80
  yeshivas and, 72–73
Epstein, Rav Yechiel Michel, 21
  on Yosel, 11
Era of the Yeshivas, 71–78
  prophets and, 71
Ethics, Torah values in, 76
Evil, 66
  Bobruisker on, 163–165
  evasive tactics of, 67–70
  perceptions of, by wicked, 68–70
  two ways of relating to, 55–56
  see also Satan

Faskowitz, Rav Chaim Boruch, 19
Fear of Heaven, Torah and, 49
Flood story, 58–60
France, Ohr Yosef network in, 39, 44
Frank, Reb Shraga, 5
Future:
  Bitachon and, 86
  focus on present vs., 79–80

Gateshead, 36
"Generals," 39
Genesis:
  Flood story in, 58–60
  Tree of Knowledge story in, 55–58
God:
  inner love of, 77–78
  justice and mercy of, 57
  man and, xviii
  reliance on, 17–18
  trust in, 9, 76–77; see also Bitachon
Gomel, 23, 28, 33
  Yozel's move of yeshiva to, 22–25
Grodzinski, Rav Chaim Ozer, 24, 43

Haggai, 71
Hakafos, 31
Halevy, Chaya, Yozel's marriage to, 8–9

# Index

Halevy, Reb Shlomo, 8
  Yozel's isolation in home of, 6–8
Halevy ben Hisdai, Rabbi Avrohom, 80
History, Novarodok philosophy of, 167–168
Honor, desire for, 17

Ibn Tibbon, Shmuel, xxi
Insecurity, 79
Isolation, 17
Israel, 39
  yeshiva founded in, 36

Jews:
  communist persecution of, 28–31, 34–35
  freed senses of, 65–66
  post-Enlightenment, 73
  Revelation at Sinai and, 64, 67
  as yevsektsia, 29
Jofen, Rav Avrohom, 25, 35, 36, 43
  Cold War telegram to, 45
  on following traditions, 37
  imprisonment of, 34
  line of fire crossed by, 33–34
  Musar study period of, 39
  overcoat of, 41
  on Rav Yozel, 105–106
  *shiurim* of, 38
Just, wicked vs., 67

Kanievsky, Rabbi Yakov, *see* Steipler
Kelm, 9

Kelm Musar, xix
Kiev, 24, 28, 33
  Novarodok yeshiva moved to, 30
*Kollelim*, 10, 12
Korkovsky, Rav Menachem, 21
Kortobin, Rav of, 5, 8
  death of, 6
Kovno, 6
Kovno Kollel, 5

Lachman, Ovadia, 10
Latvia, 36
Lavan, 84, 85, 95
"Leading the Many to Righteousness," 53, 99–101
Leib of Stvisk, Rav, 9
Levites, 66, 88–89
Levovits, Rav Yeruchom, 15, 25
Liebman, Gershon, 44
Lithuania, xv
Lubchansky, Rav Yisroel Yakov, 149–151

Magid, Rav Shraga, 161–162
Maimonides, *see* Rambam
Malachi, 71
Man:
  anger of, 57
  breaking of bad character traits by, 81
  limitations of, 76
  rushing of, 66
  shortcomings of, 50–51, 99
  will of, Torah and, 65
Marxism, 16
*Maskilim*, attempts to frame Yozel by, 8

Meltser, Rav Isser Zalman, 25
Memel, 4
Mezritch, 36
"Ministry for Religion," 29
Mir, 23
*Mivka,* 7
Moses, 34, 59, 66, 71
  Torah taught by, 70
Motivation, purity of, 17
Movshovitz, Rav Yisroel, 43, 44
Musar:
  community in, 51
  criticisms of, xv-xvi
  definition of, xv
  effects of, on religious discourse, xvii–xviii
  Kelm, xix
  Novarodok, *see* Novarodoker Musar
  personal circumstances and, xviii
  Rav Zalmanes on, 141–142
  self-awareness in, xvii–xviii
  Slobodka, xviii–xix
  Torah study and, xvii
  Vilna Gaon and, xvii
  women and, xvii

Nekrits, Rav Yehuda Leib, 22, 39
Nemitsin, 43
Nizhni-Novgorod, 24
Noach, 58–60, 154
  Avraham vs., 63
  character of, 59–60
Novarodok Battle Song, 171–172

Novarodoker Musar, xix–xxi, 12
  *birzhe* of, 16–17
  *Elul* in, 18
  emotions in, 14–15
  historiography of, 167–168
  monthly practices of, 17–18
  private property abolished in, 17
  sadness and asceticism rejected in, xx
  storming of soul in, 13–20
  struggle in, xix
  Yozel on, 19–20
Novarodok yeshiva, 11–12
  *chavuros* of, *see* Chavuros
  communist persecution of, 30–31, 33–35
  flight to Poland by, 35
  growth of, 23
  informal discussions in, 38–39
  move to Kiev by, 30
  new yeshivas founded by, 41
  organization of, 39–41
  poverty in, 41
  reidels in, 39–40
  Revolution of 1917 and, 27
  schedule of, 169–170
  Siberian exile of, 44
  typhoid epidemic and, 31
  *Va'ad Haruach,* 40
  in World War I, 22–24
  World War II and, 43–44
  yeshivas "captured" by, 24–25

Ogolnik, Rav Aharon, 39
Ohr Yosef network, 39, 44
*Omek Hadin,* 61
Opium, 55

Index

Pavlograd, 24
Photograph, perceptions of common people compared with, 65
Pinsk, 36
Poland:
  Novarodok Musar, 37–42
  in World War II, 43
  yeshivas founded in, 35–36
Polanga, 3
Pompeditha, 72
Progress, xxi
Prophets, 70–71
Purim, 18

Radun, 23
Rambam, 40
Rechovoam, 68
Reidel, 39–40
Revelation at Sinai, 64–70
Ridicule, fear of, 18
Rosatov, 24
Russian Revolution (1905), 21
Russian Revolution (1917), 27–32
  jews persecuted in, 30–32

Sadness, Novarodok Musar's rejection of, xx
Salanter, Rabbi Yisroel, xv, xvii, xviii, xix, 12, 15, 52–53, 87, 96, 168
  on storms of soul, 13
  Yozel and, 4–6
Saratov, 24, 28
Satan:
  Avraham and, 61–62, 143–144
  power of, 66

tactics of, 61
see also Evil
Seclusion, see Isolation
"Seekers," 39
Serpent, 55, 57, 64
Shaul, 68, 91
*Sheimus*, xix
Shell games, 66
Shem, 64
Shenker, Rav Avrohom, 5
Shimanovits, Rav Mordechai, 153–154
*shiurim*, 38
Shkop, Rav Shimon, 38
Shmuel, 68, 91
Shmulevitz, Rav Chaim, on Novarodok yeshivas, 38–39
Shtein, Yakov, 3–4
Siberia, exile of Novarodok yeshivas to, 44
Simcha Zissel Ziv, Rav, xix, 7, 15
  Yozel's friendship with, 9–10
Simiatits, 36
Sinai, Revelation at, 64–70
Slobodka, Yozel's move to, 6
Slobodka Musar, xviii–xix, 12, 23
Slutsk, 25
Solomon, King, 75
Soloveitchik, Chaim, 12
Soloveitchik, Rabbi Yosef Dov, 5
Soul, storming of, 13–20
Spector, Rav Yitshak Elchonon, 7, 10
Stalin, Josef, 34
Steipler, 34, 38, 39
  escape from Russia by, 35

Struggle, in Novarodok Musar, xix
Succos, 18
Sura, 72

*Taanis Dibur*, 17
Talmud, 40
Tarshish, Rav Zelig, 6
Tchernigov, 24
*Tefillin*, 29
Tel Aviv, 36
"Tenth is Holy," 39
Torah:
    combining cultural assumptions with, 79–80
    distractions from, 51
    ethics and, 76
    Fear of Heaven and, 49
    good character as key to, 50–51
    grandeur of, 49–50, xvi
    joy and happiness provided by, 77
    man's judgment vs., 76–77
    on removal of natural biases from intellect, 65
    will and, 65
*Torah Lishmo*, xvi
Torah study, xv–xvii
    Chaim of Volozhin on, xvi–xvii
    character and, xvi
    excuses for avoidance of, 100–101
    Musar vs., xvii
    women and, xvii
Tower of Bavel, 158
Tree of Knowlege story, 55–58
    Adam's choice in, 56–57
    nakedness in, 57–58

Trotsky, Lev, 33
Trust in God, 76–77
    *see also* Bitachon
Tsaritsin, 24
Tsirinsky, Reb Gershon, 9

Ukraine, 22

*Va'ad Haruach*, 40
Valdshein, Rav Yitzhak Elchonon, 20, 39, 157–160
Veintrob, Rav Shmuel, 36
Vilna, World War II flight to, 43
Vilna Gaon:
    Lithuanian Jewery and, xvi
    Musar and, xvii
Vitkind, Rav Hillel, 36
Volozhiner, Rav Chaim, 43

Warsaw, 36
Wicked:
    just vs., 67
    perceptions of evil by, 68–70
Will, Torah and, 65
Women, Musar and, xvii
World War I, 22–24, 73
World War II, Poland in, 43

Yakov, 84–85
    Eisav's birthright purchased by, 93–95
    Yitshak's blessing and, 93–97
Yanai, Rabbi, 49
Yeshivas:
    Bolshevik persecution of, 28–30
    complete men produced by, 72
    Enlightenment and, 72–73

Index

founded by Yozel, 9
founded in Poland, 35–36
Novarodok, *see* Novarodok yeshiva
renewal of, modern world vs., 73–75
Yevsektsia, 28–29
Yisro, 70
Yitshak, 62, 95
   blessing of, 93–97
   sacrifice of, 62–63
Yoizel, Rav, 16
Yom Kippur, 40
Yona, Rav, 40
Yosef, 85, 86
Yozel, Rav Yosef, 17, 53
   on *birzhe*, 16
   coded messages sent by, 28
   death of, 31–32, 33
   on difficulty of Novarodok Musar, 19–20
   effects of 1905 Revolution on, 21
   Epstein on, 11
   historiography of, 167–168
   isolation of, 6–8, 9, 10
   *kollelim* founded by, 10, 12
   lectern of, 6
   legacy of, 32, 33, 105–123
   marriage of, 8–9
   as meteor, 22
   Novarodok yeshiva moved to Kiev by, 30
   rescue of grave of, 45
   revolution of 1917 and, 28
   sayings of, 125–139
   Simcha Zissel Ziv's friendship with, 9–10
   Slobodka move of, 6
   Spector's message to, 7
   translating writings of, xxi–xxii
   trust in God by, 9
   wanderings of, 6
   yeshivas founded by, 9, 11–12
   yeshivas named after, 36
Yozel Hurvitz, Rabbi Yosef:
   business of, 4–5
   life of, 3–10
   personality of, 3

Zaitchik, Rav Chaim, 39
Zalmanes, Rav Avrohom, 36, 141–142
Zalman Ziv, Rabbi Shlomo, 3
Zechariah, 71
Zeldovitz, Reb Dov, 12
Zundel of Salant, Reb, xvii

## About the Author

Dr. Meir Levin was born in Vilnius, Lithuania, where he first heard of Novarodok Musar. He came to New York at a young age to pursue religious and secular studies. He studied at Yeshiva Rabbi Samson Raphael Hirsch, Yeshiva University, Beth Midrash Gavoah-Lakewood Rabbinical College, and obtained his medical degree from Downstate College of Medicine, New York. He has been gathering material about Novarodok for fifteen years. During this time he has been able to meet and study with some of the surviving disciples of this movement. Dr. Levin is currently in the academic practice of hematology and oncology and lives with his wife and children in Queens, New York.

www.ingramcontent.com/pod-product-compliance
Lightning Source LLC
Chambersburg PA
CBHW021124300426
44113CB00006B/283